Buddhists and Christians

FAITH MEETS FAITH

An Orbis Series in Interreligious Dialogue
Paul F. Knitter and William R. Burrows, General Editors
Editorial Advisors
John Berthrong
Diana Eck
Karl-Josef Kuschel
Lamin Sanneh
George E. Tinker
Felix Wilfred

In the contemporary world, the many religions and spiritualities stand in need of greater communication and cooperation. More than ever before, they must speak to, learn from, and work with each other in order to maintain their vital identities and to contribute to fashioning a better world.

The FAITH MEETS FAITH Series seeks to promote interreligious dialogue by providing an open forum for exchange among followers of different religious paths. While the Series wants to encourage creative and bold responses to questions arising from contemporary appreciations of religious plurality, it also recognizes the multiplicity of basic perspectives concerning the methods and content of interreligious dialogue.

Although rooted in a Christian theological perspective, the Series does not limit itself to endorsing any single school of thought or approach. By making available to both the scholarly community and the general public works that represent a variety of religious and methodological viewpoints, FAITH MEETS FAITH seeks to foster an encounter among followers of the religions of the world on matters of common concern.

FAITH MEETS FAITH SERIES

Buddhists and Christians

Through Comparative Theology to Solidarity

James L. Fredericks

ORBIS BOOKS

Maryknoll, New York 10545

Founded in 1970, Orbis Books endeavors to publish works that enlighten the mind, nourish the spirit, and challenge the conscience. The publishing arm of the Maryknoll Fathers and Brothers, Orbis seeks to explore the global dimensions of the Christian faith and mission, to invite dialogue with diverse cultures and religious traditions, and to serve the cause of reconciliation and peace. The books published reflect the opinions of their authors and are not meant to represent the official position of the Maryknoll Society. To obtain more information about Maryknoll and Orbis Books, please visit our website at www.maryknoll.org.

Manuscript editing and typesetting by Joan Weber Laflamme.
Manufactured in the United States of America.

Library of Congress Cataloging-in-Publication Data

Fredericks, James L. (James Leo), 1951–
  Buddhists and Christians : through comparative theology to solidarity
/ James L. Fredericks.
    p. cm. — (Faith meets faith series)
  Includes bibliographical references and index.
  ISBN 1-57075-555-8
  1. Christianity and other religions—Buddhism. 2.
Buddhism—Relations—Christianity. I. Title. II. Faith meets faith.
  BR128.B8F74 2004
  261.2'43—dc22
                                        2004006502

For Megan, Martin, and Kate

Contents

Introduction

In late summer 2001, I welcomed to Loyola Marymount University in Los Angeles, where I teach, a group of Pure Land Buddhists from Japan. We were gathering for a week of friendship and dialogue. In the days we had together before the formal dialogue meetings began, we visited various Buddhist and Catholic communities in the Los Angeles area. On the last day of our week together, we had planned to watch Ichiro Suzuki, a popular figure in Japan as well as the United States, play in Anaheim stadium. That baseball game, however, would be canceled—and not because of rain. The first day of dialogue was given to a discussion of how theological renewal in the Roman Catholic Church led eventually to institutional reform. My Buddhist guests were keenly interested in the theological thinking that led to the Second Vatican Council and the religious renewal that came out of it. They wanted to know how this might be an impetus to the renewal of their own Buddhist community in Japan. This discussion came to an abrupt end the following morning, Tuesday, September 11, 2001.

On the evening of the terrorist attacks the campus ministry staff at my university organized a mass. A special invitation was extended to our Buddhists guests, and a place was reserved for them at the front of the chapel. The Buddhists were quite moved by the psalm we sang that evening: "Shepherd me, O Lord, beyond my wants, beyond my fears, from death into life." This Old Testament text became a focus for our conversations in the days that followed. My Buddhist friends, of course, responded to the words of the psalmist from their own religious perspective. Since the Buddha taught that desire brings about suffering, the image of being led to a place beyond wants and fears resonated very deeply with my guests.

An act of terror gathered us around this psalm. In sharing our "wants" and "fears," to say nothing of our very different understandings of being "shepherded," Buddhists and Christians learned much from one another. Without exaggeration, I can say that we Buddhists and Christians formed a new kind of community in those days we spent with one another after the terrorist attacks. In this community Christians continue to follow the path of Christ and Buddhists continue to follow the Buddha's *dharma*. In fact, I think all of us would say that our religious commitments have been strengthened by our communal ties to one another. What makes us a community is our desire to learn from one another. The Buddhists came to learn from Christians about theological renewal and institutional reform. As things turned out, they also learned about how Christians imagine being shepherded beyond their wants and fears, "from death into life." And, as things turned out, the Christian participants at this dialogue meeting learned great things from the Buddhists about wanting and fearing. Christians also learned that Pure

Land Buddhists do not think of a passage from death into life, but rather a passage from death into birth—birth in the Pure Land of Amida Buddha.

Almost half a century ago the great Indian philosopher Radhakrishnan began to write about what today has come to be called globalization. Recognizing that the colonial rituals of cultural dominance and submission were quickly passing, he noted, "For the first time in the history of our planet, its inhabitants have become one whole, each and every part of which is affected by the fortunes of every other." Radhakrishnan went on to lament, "And yet the sense that mankind must become a community is still a casual whim, a vague aspiration, not generally accepted as a conscious ideal or an urgent practical necessity moving us to feel the dignity of a common citizenship and the call of a common duty."[1]

Radhakrishnan could have written these words today as a commentary on the state of the world after the terrorist attacks of 9/11. Besides its economic consequences, globalization brings religious believers into contact with one another, for better or worse, in ways that no religious community could have imagined in the past. Contact, however, is not community. Religiously motivated violence around the world bears dreadful testimony to this fact. Globalization erodes the traditional bond that links a religion to a specific locale. Religion has always been linked with territory. Europe was a "Christendom." Islam's *Dar Es Salam* (House of Peace) stretched from Morocco in the west to Mindanao in the east. The Hindu *Dharma-raj* (Kingdom of True Teachings) spanned the Indian subcontinent. There were, of course, religious minorities in all these areas, but these minorities lived in territory defined by the religious worldview of the majority. Now, fifteen million Muslims live in secular Europe and almost half of all Koreans are Christians. Africa is neither Christian nor Muslim "space" today, but rather a place where Christians and Muslims must learn to live peaceably with one another. In Latin America Roman Catholics rub shoulders with Evangelical and Pentecostal Christians as well as pre-Columbian traditions. Violence against minority religious communities is seen in countries as different as India, Indonesia, Sri Lanka, Nigeria, and Egypt.

The United States, of course, has its own stories to tell. Diana Eck claims that it is now the most religiously diverse country in the world.[2] Since the enactment of the Immigration and Naturalization Act of 1965, immigrants have brought Islam from Iran and Pakistan; Buddhism from Thailand, Vietnam, and Cambodia; and unfamiliar forms of Christianity from Korea, Egypt, the Philippines, and Vietnam. For Americans, religious diversity used to mean yarmulkes and cassocks. Now it means head-scarves and saffron robes, turbans, and the *navjote* (the thread worn by Zoroastrians). In light of this challenge, we need to cultivate new forms of social solidarity with neighbors who follow other religious paths. Some years ago Buddhists from Taiwan wanted to build a temple in Hacienda Heights, California but encountered roadblocks from Los Angeles County. Jews, Christians, and others joined together to testify on their behalf at the zoning hearing. Minnesota's Mall of America has its own interfaith council. When a vandal threw a rock through a window displaying a menorah in Bozeman, Montana, Christian leaders exhorted their people to display menorahs in their own windows. Overnight, menorahs appeared all over the city in solidarity with

Bozeman's tiny Jewish community. A community of Methodists in Fremont, California, that wants to build a new church and a local community of Muslims that wants to build a new mosque have discovered that they can solve their real estate, zoning, and financial problems by building on the same parcel of land.

Examples of social solidarity, like the effort of Christians to assist Buddhists in the building of the temple in Los Angeles County, are greatly to be praised. Christians, however, need to take this a step further by establishing new forms of religious solidarity with other religious communities as well. The time is quickly coming, and indeed has already arrived in some parts of the world, when Christians will no longer be able to make sense of their own religious lives apart from an understanding-in-depth of the religious lives of their neighbors who follow other religious paths. Social solidarity calls Christians to work cooperatively with other religious believers for the betterment of the wider community. The religious solidarity called for today requires Christians to look on their neighbors who follow other religious paths not merely with tolerance, praiseworthy as it is. Tolerance can be a form of indifference. The proximity of religious communities to one another today makes such indifference harder to maintain. The religious solidarity called for today requires Christians to go beyond tolerance in order to look on their neighbors who follow other religious paths with the esteem and gratitude reserved for faithful friends and cherished teachers. By learning about other religions in depth, Christians will be in a position to think about their own religious lives with new insight. In the process, Christians will begin to look on other religions less as a threat than as a valued resource for their own spiritual enrichment. Out of this will come a new sense of religious solidarity with those who follow other religious paths.

The twenty-first century will not witness the birth of a global religion that will supersede Buddhism and Christianity, Islam and Hinduism, Daoism and Confucianism and Judaism. In fact, the contrary may well be the case. The nation state calls us to a civic identity as citizens of the United States, Nigeria, France, or India. As globalization erodes this civic identity, religious identity becomes more important. In many parts of the world religion is taking the place of Cold War ideologies as an organizing principle in the new global order—and disorder.[3] As religious identity and affiliation begin to eclipse national identity and citizenship, conflict between religious communities comes as no surprise. In the interest of peace, religious believers have a responsibility to build bridges of cooperation and respect that link their religion with the religion of others. The social solidarity that interreligious cooperation promotes needs to be augmented by a religious solidarity as well. Not only should Christian believers work together with those who follow other religious paths for the betterment of humanity, but Christians need to open themselves to other religious believers in such a way that the other religions come to be seen as a genuine spiritual resource for living more faithfully the path of Christ.

I want to make a case for interreligious dialogue as a way to promote a new religious solidarity. My friend Dharma Master Hsin-tao of Taiwan is organizing dialogues among Buddhists and Muslims around the world in order to increase understanding and establish bonds of friendship among those who follow the

Buddha's Middle Path and those who walk the Prophet's Straight Path. Since the Second Vatican Council, Roman Catholics have initiated formal dialogues with Buddhists, Muslims, Hindus, Jews, and others in many parts of the world. Interreligious dialogue is a way for Christians to discover in the other religious paths truths that are enriching and transforming. In this process dialogue with other believers gives rise to solidarity—the genuinely religious solidarity called for in the future. More specifically, this book seeks to show how much Christians can learn by entering into dialogue with Buddhists, and how, in the process of learning from one another, Buddhists and Christians can forge new bonds of solidarity for the benefit of all. The little community of Buddhists and Christians thrown together by their "wants" and "fears" as a result of the terrorist attacks of 9/11 is but a simple example of the religious solidarity fostered by interreligious dialogue I want to explore.

In making a case for interreligious dialogue as a form of solidarity, this book is also an example of comparative theology. Doing theology comparatively means crossing over into the world of another religious believer and learning the truths that animate the life of that believer. Doing theology comparatively also means coming back to Christianity transformed by these truths, now able to ask new questions about Christian faith and its meaning for today. Doing theology in dialogue with Buddhists means that Christians will have to learn something about Buddhism on its own terms, not as Christians would wedge Buddhism into their own religious beliefs. Buddhists do not worry about going to heaven. They certainly do not wonder if the Buddha was inspired by the Holy Spirit. These are questions Christians have about Buddhists prior to meeting them and learning from them. In crossing over into Buddhism, these questions will be left behind. Buddhists have a whole new set of questions for Christians to ask. In the process of asking these new questions, Christians will come to look on their friendships with Buddhists as precious indeed.

I do comparative theology in conversation with Buddhism. Buddhism has wonderful things to teach Christians. With the help of my Buddhist friends, like those Pure Land Buddhists who shared so much of their Buddhist faith in the days after 9/11, I have been crossing over into the Buddha's *dharma* for many years now. My Buddhist friends have been skillful teachers and tireless in their efforts to benefit me. Like so many other Christians who have entered into dialogue with Buddhists, I can say without qualification that my Christian faith has been enriched by my friendships with those who follow the Middle Path. Buddhist truths allow us to ask new questions of Christian faith and enrich our understanding of the path of Christ.

The need for new forms of religious solidarity raises the problem of the "theology of religions" today. Religions like Hinduism and Islam, Buddhism and Judaism have evolved over the centuries into enormously elaborate explanatory systems. Tradition supplies Christians with their own way of making sense out of the world. This includes ways of making sense out of the puzzle-pieces of religious diversity. The theology of religions is the branch of Christian thought that tries to explain the status and meaning of other religious traditions based on the teachings of Christianity. Today, no theology of religions is adequate to the needs of the Christian community. I have taken this position in regard to the so-called pluralist theology of religions elsewhere.[4] In the present book I look in detail at what is variously called the fulfillment or inclusivist theology of religions. In this approach to religious diversity the other religious paths are seen as lesser expressions of the same saving truth witnessed to explicitly and fully by Christianity. The time has come to put aside the quest for an adequate theology of religions. All candidates for such a theology, including fulfillment theologies, allow Christians to deal with religious diversity without ever having to leave the comfortable armchair of Christian belief. I propose that Christians get up out of the armchair and cross over into another religious tradition.

The first chapter of the book has to do with the remarkable development among Roman Catholics over the last fifty years of a fulfillment model for a theology of religions. In contrast to the pluralist and exclusivist approaches, a fulfillment theology of religions succeeds best in meeting the demands of Christian belief. Despite this, the fulfillment model is still not adequate to the needs of Christians believers today. The urgency of religious diversity today demands new forms of religious solidarity. Christianity's fulfillment approach is not up to this task. This is what I argue in the first chapter.

Doing Christian theology comparatively, in dialogue with Buddhism, means that Christians have to know something about Buddhism on its own terms. This is the point of the second and third chapters. Of course, I do not presume to say anything exhaustive about Buddhism in so short a space. Instead, I take on a much more modest goal. Eventually I will explore the meaning of God using the Buddhist notion of emptiness. In order to appreciate Buddhist emptiness, however, it will be helpful to learn something of the basic teachings of early Buddhism, especially the silence of the Buddha. The second chapter explores the Buddha's silence and what it reveals about the most basic teachings of Buddhism. The third chapter discusses in depth the Buddhist notion of emptiness *(sunyata)* as taught by Nagarjuna (c. AD 150), one of the most influential teachers in the entire history of Buddhism.

With the silence of the Buddha and the principle of emptiness as background, we will be able to use what we have learned from Buddhism in order to think about Christianity in new ways. In the fourth chapter I use Buddhist emptiness as a guide for thinking about God. In effect, this chapter is a kind of dialogue between Thomas Aquinas (1225–74) and Nagarjuna. Like other Christians, Aquinas believes that God is incomprehensible. In dialogue with Nagarjuna, however, we begin to see how unusual Aquinas's view of God's incomprehensibility really is. This will open up the possibility of seeing both similarities and differences between Buddhism and Christianity. The fifth chapter reflects on how doing theology in dialogue with Buddhism contributes to building new forms of social and religious solidarity that will benefit the world today.

Doing theology comparatively requires Christians to cross over into the world of their Buddhist friends. Therefore, I need to acknowledge some of my Buddhist teachers. In Kyoto, special thanks go to Masao Abe, who has taught me so much for over twenty years about Buddhist emptiness and God. Thanks also to Ryusei Takeda of Ryukoku University in Kyoto and the students in his seminar on Buddhism and culture. Maria and Ruben Habito shared many ideas with me while we worked together in Kyoto with occasional visits to Taiwan. In Dazaifu, Japan, Dennis Hirota and his colleagues at Chikushi Joshi Gakuen University have taught me much about dialogue and solidarity. In Los Angeles I must mention the late Venerable Dr. Havanpola Ratanasara and all the members, Buddhist and Christian, of the Buddhist-Christian dialogue group. Thanks also goes to Hope Blacker, Linda Shultz, and Barbara Murphy for their constructive comments. At Orbis Books, thanks go to Bill Burrows, who encouraged me to write this book and supported its completion. Finally, thanks go to all those involved in the Fulbright Program for their support of my research in Kyoto.

1

The Catholic Church
and the Other Religions

Karl Rahner, SJ, did not overestimate the magnitude of the problem posed by the diversity of religions to Christianity today when he wrote that the pluralism of religions

> is a greater threat and a reason for greater unrest for Christianity than for any other religion. For no other religion—not even Islam—maintains so absolutely that it is *the* religion, the one and only valid revelation of the one living God, as does the Christian religion. The fact of the pluralism of religions, which endures and still from time to time becomes virulent . . . even after a history of 2000 years, must therefore be the greatest scandal and the greatest vexation for Christianity.[1]

At the center of Christianity's vexation and by far the major reason religious diversity poses such a serious challenge to Christians is Christianity's faith in Jesus Christ as the unique and universal savior, the Word of God that has come into the world for the salvation of all. For this reason Christian thinking about non-Christians and their religions struggles with a double affirmation. First, Christians have believed that salvation is always in some way salvation in the name of Jesus Christ. "I am the way, and the truth, and the life," Jesus announces in the Gospel of John, before going on to say, "no one comes to the Father, but by me" (Jn 14:6). But this focus on the uniqueness of the historical Jesus does not stand alone. There is also Christian teaching concerning the universality of God's saving grace. "I now see how true it is that God has no favorites," Peter preaches in the Acts of the Apostles, "but that in every nation, the man who is godfearing and does what is right is acceptable to him" (Acts 10:34–35). Thus a considerable tension is built into the Christian tradition itself regarding the meaning of other religious traditions. If all salvation is in Jesus Christ, are all those who do not profess the Christian faith damned? Or is it that those who follow other religious paths have an implicit faith sufficient for salvation? If other believers do have such an implicit faith, are these believers saved through the wisdom and moral virtue of their religions or despite these religions?

Over roughly the last fifty years Roman Catholic thinking about the meaning and status of other religious traditions has undergone a dramatic development.

1

The central authority of the Roman Catholic Church responded to the rise of the modern world, with its pluralism and relativism, with suspicion and denial. The Catholic Church's missionary effort, on the other hand, was undeniably entangled with the modern world's colonial system. The Second Vatican Council (1962–65), called at the very end of the colonial era, brought about a major change in the Catholic Church's relationship with the modern world.[2] That a major theme at the council would be the meaning and status of the religious lives of Confucians, Hindus, Buddhists, Muslims, and Jews should come as no surprise.

In the last fifty years the Catholic Church has turned away from a negative view of the other religious paths as darkness and deviltry. In their official teachings Catholics look with esteem on the other paths as part of God's encompassing plan for the salvation of all creation. The Catholic Church, in its official documents at least, does not look on the other religious traditions as sources of salvation in their own right. All salvation is in Christ, who works most visibly in the Christian community and relatively less visibly outside of it. Moreover, the religious aspirations of all human beings are fulfilled by Christ, the one savior of the whole world. The other religious traditions are related "in various ways," according to the Roman Catholic Church, to the great mediation of grace which is Christ and which has been established historically in the church. The Roman Catholic approach to the other religions, therefore, has been called a "fulfillment theology."[3] This chapter traces some of the highlights of the Catholic Church's turn to a fulfillment model for thinking about its relationship with other religious traditions.

THE SECOND VATICAN COUNCIL

Much has been written about the Second Vatican Council and its understanding of other religious traditions.[4] Here, I wish only to highlight some of the background issues that are visible in the council documents. Where previous official statements of the Roman Catholic Church were tentative, the Second Vatican Council is clear and unambiguous about the possibility that those who follow other religious paths can be saved in Christ by the grace of the Holy Spirit. However, the council documents leave unresolved the role, if any, that the religious paths themselves might play in God's plan of salvation. For example, is a Buddhist saved by Christ despite his or her Buddhist religious life or by means of it? In regard to the way in which such people are saved, the council maintains a carefully crafted ambiguity and restraint. The roots of the council's ambiguity lead back into pre-conciliar developments within the Roman Catholic thinking about other religions. The work of Jean Daniélou, SJ, and Karl Rahner, SJ, is especially noteworthy in this regard.[5]

Daniélou published regularly on the meaning and status of the various religious paths from 1956 until 1973.[6] His approach to the question is governed by his understanding of God's revelation in history. In Daniélou's view, all of history is the progressive revelation of God to humankind. Within this general view of the history of the world, salvation history proper begins with Abraham and reaches its apex in Jesus Christ, whose saving presence within history is now continued by the church. This means that Daniélou sees a fundamental distinction between Judaism and Christianity, on the one hand, and all the other religions on the other. Buddhism and Hinduism are "natural religions." By this he means that they are the product of ordinary human creativity. Judaism and Christianity are "supernatural religions." These religions are the result not only of human creativity but also of God's special activity within history:

> The essential difference between Catholicism and all other religions is that the others start from man. They are touching and often very beautiful attempts, rising very high in their search for God. But in Catholicism there is a contrary movement, the descent of God towards the world, in order to communicate his life to it.[7]

Natural religions like Buddhism and Islam have their own proper autonomy and are worthy of respect. However, God has ordained that these religions find their ultimate fulfillment in Christ, the apex of history, and in Christianity, the supernatural religion of Christ.[8]

The influence of Daniélou's theology of religions can be seen in the council documents. For example, *Ad gentes (AG)* speaks of the other religious paths as endeavors in which people "search for God, groping for Him that they may by chance find Him" and as human initiatives that "need to be enlightened and purified" by the gospel. Even so, the other religious paths are not evil or worthless, for they can "sometimes serve as pedagogy toward the true God or as a preparation for the gospel" and thus find their fulfillment there (*AG,* no. 3; see also *Lumen gentium* [*LG*], no. 23).

Karl Rahner, SJ, was also widely influential at the Second Vatican Council. Along with Daniélou, Rahner understands religious diversity as a progressive unfolding of revelation within history in which Christ forms the summit. In this respect, Rahner's theology of religions, like Daniélou's, is also a fulfillment theology.[9] In contrast to Daniélou, however, Rahner does not make so strict a distinction between natural and supernatural religions. Human beings are never utter strangers to divine grace. God's grace is always at work in all human beings, no matter who they are. Moreover, this supernatural grace is manifest in the visible forms of human creativity. Because of this, Rahner comes to a significantly different assessment of the role and meaning of the different religions:

> In view of the social nature of man, however, it is quite unthinkable that man, being what he is, could actually achieve this relationship to God . . . in an absolutely private interior reality and this outside of the actual religious bodies which offer themselves to him in the environment in which he lives.[10]

The other religions cannot be seen as merely natural expressions of human wisdom and aspiration, as with Daniélou. The religious practices of Muslims and

Jains, Confucians and Buddhists are concrete expressions of God's supernatural grace to those who follow these religious paths. As such, other religions do not merely prepare human beings to hear the gospel *(preparatio evangelii)*, they are supernatural acts of God that makes saving grace available to human beings.

Rahner's theology of religions can be seen in the council documents as well. According to *Ad gentes*, "The universal design of God for the salvation of the human race is not carried out exclusively in people's souls, with a kind of secrecy" (no. 3). Rahner argued that grace always takes visible and tangible social forms. Council statements such as this should not be overestimated, however. They move in a Rahnerian direction to the extent that they recognize a supernatural grace to be already operative and efficacious in the lives of people who are not Christians. They do not go as far as Rahner would in recognizing the other religious paths themselves as mediations of Christ's salvation.

The documents of the Second Vatican Council reflect an understanding of religious diversity in which Christianity fulfills the religious aspirations of human beings reflected in the many religions of the world. The documents are indebted in various degrees to the theologies of both Daniélou and Rahner, without any attempt to reconcile them. Pope John Paul II, who has done more than any pope in history to forge new relationships with those who follow other religious paths, has taken the council as a point of departure for his own teaching.

JOHN PAUL II

John Paul II is not only the first pope in history to visit a synagogue, he is also the first pope to stand at the Wailing Wall in Jerusalem and pray. This pope's outreach to Jews and other religious believers is placed on a clear theological foundation. Since the first year of his papacy, John Paul II has responded to the reality of religious diversity by turning to a theology of the Holy Spirit.

The pope's interest in the Holy Spirit can be seen in his first encyclical letter, *Redemptor hominis (RH),* written in 1979. He has continued to develop since then toward a greater appreciation of those who follow other religious paths and their religions. In section six of the encyclical, the pope recognizes in the beliefs of others an "effect of the Spirit of truth operating outside the visible confines of the Mystical Body." In a radio broadcast from Manila the pope focused on the presence of the Holy Spirit in all authentic prayer, a theme that would eventually bear fruit in the famous meeting of religious leaders with the pope at Assisi.[11]

Shortly after returning from a trip to India, the pope promulgated another encyclical letter, *Dominum et vivificantem* (1986). In section fifty-three of this letter John Paul II teaches that the action of the Holy Spirit cannot be limited to the church. Christians "must hold that the Holy Spirit offers to all the possibility of being associated, in a way known to God, with the Pascal Mystery." In this encyclical John Paul II has gone beyond Daniélou's framework for interpreting the theological meaning of other religious paths. Has the pope thereby taken a Rahnerian turn? Section 28 of this encyclical notes the Spirit's presence "at the very source of the human person's existential and religious questioning." The human quest for God is never completely "natural." And like Rahner's theology of religions, the pope does not restrict the activity of the Spirit to the purely interior, private realm of the individual. "The Spirit's presence and activity affect not only individuals but also society and history, peoples, cultures and religions."

In keeping with the fulfillment approach of both Daniélou and Rahner, the pope nowhere suggests that other religious paths are salvific in their own right. All salvation is in Christ. Through the working of the Holy Spirit in the religions, salvation in Christ is available to all. Neither does the pope suggest that the church can be completely distinguished from Christ and the Spirit. Instead, John Paul II speaks of "participated forms of mediation," that is, the participation of the other religions in the saving mystery of Christ, which is fully present in the church.

John Paul II's phrase "participated forms of mediation" can be traced back to *Lumen gentium*: "The unique mediation of the Redeemer does not exclude, but rather gives rise to a manifold cooperation which is but a participation in this one source" (no. 62). This conciliar text does not speak of the other religions per se, but rather of elements in the spiritual and material situation of other religious believers. In *Redemptoris missio* John Paul II makes use of this principle in asserting the centrality of Christ in the salvation of all: "Although participated forms of mediation of different kinds and degrees are not excluded, they acquire meaning and value *only* from Christ's own mediation, and they cannot be understood as parallel or complementary to his" (no. 5). Religions are not equal. Religions are not relative. There are not many kinds of salvation. There is but one salvation, and the Holy Spirit calls all men and women to one visible community, the church. Even so, the Holy Spirit is not a stranger to Muslims and Buddhists, Jains and Daoists. The great mediation of grace, which is Christ, can be discerned in the religious lives of those who follow other religious paths.

THE ASIAN CHURCHES

In addition to the contributions of John Paul II, there are bishops and theologians serving local churches in Asian countries like India and the Philippines who are making a significant contribution to Roman Catholic views of religious diversity. For the churches of Asia, religious diversity is by no means a theoretical matter. Even in the Philippines, where a large majority of the population is Roman Catholic, there is a significant Muslim population. In places like Sri Lanka, Indonesia, China, Japan, and India, Christians are a tiny minority where religions like Islam, Hinduism, Confucianism, Daoism, and Buddhism are intimately associated with ancient cultural achievements and even national identity. Many theologians and bishops in the Asian churches have recognized the need to develop local theologies for responding to the pastoral needs of their people. In some cases this has meant a strong commitment to interreligious dialogue and attempts to move beyond the council and the subsequent Roman statements. The documents of the Federation of Asian Bishops' Councils (FABC)[12] and the work of prominent Indian theologians such as Michael Amaladoss, Felix Wilfred, Aloysius Pieris, and Virginia Fabella are noteworthy examples.[13] More than any other Asian theologian, however, Jacques Dupuis has distinguished himself for his work in the area of the theology of religions.

Jacques Dupuis, a Belgian, has spent much of his life as a Jesuit priest serving the church in India. Although Dupuis has a command of Roman documents and theological developments in the West, his theological approach to religious diversity is deeply molded by the life of the church in India. To lose track of this fact would be to misunderstand much about this man's contribution to the whole church. The Second Vatican Council opened up the possibility of accepting other religious traditions as "ways" or "paths" of salvation. John Paul II has confirmed this view with his teaching since the council. Dupuis wants to move beyond the notion that the aspirations of all religious believers are fulfilled in Christianity without jettisoning Christianity's core affirmation of Jesus Christ as the unique savior of all. In this respect Dupuis wants to address the weaknesses of fulfillment theologies without falling into the error of religious relativism that marks the pluralist model proposed by philosophers like John Hick.[14] The pluralist model and the theologies of religions based on it reject Christianity's traditional claim that Jesus Christ is the one and only savior of all. In the pluralist paradigm Christianity is but one interpretation of an ultimately unnameable transcendent reality. Every religion has its own interpretation of this transcendent reality. There is nothing unique or normative about Jesus Christ. All religions are of equal value as separate paths to salvation. Christ is but one way to name this salvation. In contrast to the pluralist approach, Dupuis makes a double affirmation: Christians must continue to affirm the centrality of Jesus Christ in the salvation of all, and at the same time, they must recognize the soteriological value of the other religious paths:

> Jesus Christ is indeed the constitutive Savior of humankind, and the Christ event is the cause of the salvation of all human beings; but this does not prevent the other traditions from serving as "mediations" of the mystery of salvation in Jesus Christ for their followers within God's design for humankind.[15]

In making this double affirmation Dupuis is drawing on not only the lived experience of his local church in India but also the teachings of John Paul II. When he mentions "mediations," Dupuis has *Redemptoris hominis* in mind, where the pope introduces his key idea that other religious traditions may be looked on as "participated forms of mediation" (no. 5).

Dupuis, however, wants to move beyond the fulfillment theology established in the official documents. In the fulfillment schema those who follow other religious paths are truly touched by the saving power of Christ and the Spirit by means of the paths, but their deepest religious aspirations find fulfillment only in Christianity and explicit faith in Christ. Dupuis wants to affirm a "religious pluralism in principle."[16]

In this regard, Dupuis makes three points. First, he argues that God has been revealed to human beings throughout the entire history of the human race. Unlike Daniélou, however, Dupuis rejects the notion of a "special" history of salvation beginning with Abraham and ending in Jesus Christ. As God established a covenant with the Jews, God has made other covenants with human beings in many times and many places. As the covenant with the Jews is not abrogated in the "new and everlasting" covenant made in Christ, so also God's bond with those who follow the many religious paths of the world is not provisional, abolished or revoked by the death and resurrection of Jesus Christ.[17] Second, Christ must always be located within God's wider global plan to save all of creation. Jesus Christ is "unquestionably the center, the apex, high point, and interpretive key" of God's plan.[18] The Christ event, however, must not be isolated from the worldwide drama of salvation as if it could stand alone, apart from the plan as a whole. Jesus of Nazareth does not completely represent God's action in the world and does not exhaust God's saving power. "Rather, the historic (and as such particular) saving event of Jesus Christ leaves room for a saving action by God, through his Word and his Spirit, that goes beyond even the risen humanity of the incarnate Word."[19] Third, Christians must recognize that God's way of working in the world is pluralistic in principle. The Holy Spirit has raised up the religious traditions of the world to provide human beings with paths to salvation. Christians must recognize Hinduism and Islam, Buddhism and Confucianism, the indigenous religions and the other paths as "gifts of God to the peoples of the world."[20] Moreover, this pluralism is not just to be tolerated but to be welcomed by Christian believers as a grace from God and an integral part of God's plan.

The many religious traditions are related by means of a kind of complementarity. Religious paths are complementary to Christianity in that they enshrine truths that are not known within Christian tradition. This is to suggest that "the Christ" is revealed in Hinduism in ways that is not the case in Christianity, which is focused on the historical Jesus. Therefore, if Christians seek to know the depths of God, they must search out these depths by turning their attention to the way God is revealed in other religious traditions. The revelation of God in Christ does not cancel out the other paths but confirms them. Christ brings the drama of salvation to its culmination "not by way of substitution or replacement, but through confirmation and accomplishment."[21] Therefore, the other paths have not been raised up by the Holy Spirit only to be integrated or assumed into Christianity or absorbed by it. They are intended by God for the salvation of souls and enjoy their own autonomy apart from Christianity.

The centrality of the church's hope in the kingdom of God forms an important part of Dupuis's understanding of other religions. In this respect his theological contribution has much in common with that of other Asian theologians and bishops. Theologians who are "regnocentric," or centered on Jesus' proclamation of the kingdom of God, recognize that all human beings who work for justice and harmony—signs of the kingdom of God announced by Jesus Christ—are heirs to God's kingdom and thus saved. These theologians focus on the elements within other religions that promote an "integral liberation" and therefore call for Christians to collaborate with other religious believers in the building of societies that are just and harmonious.

Following Vatican II and various statements of the FABC, regnocentric theologians emphasize that the reign of God cannot be identified with the church unambiguously. The universality of the kingdom of God requires Christians to recognize that the kingdom is present wherever gospel values are present. This means that Christians should expect to find the kingdom emerging outside the boundaries of the church. For Jacques Dupuis,

> the religious traditions contribute, in a mysterious way, to the building up of the Reign of God among their followers and in the world. They exercise, for their own members, a certain mediation of the Kingdom—doubtless different from that which is operative in the church—even if it is difficult to define this mediation with theological precision.[22]

If the church cannot simply be identified with the kingdom, is membership in the church necessary for salvation? In answering this question Dupuis recommends avoiding two extremes. One extreme would be to place the necessity and universality of the church on the same level as that of Christ. This would be tantamount to a return to the outdated principle "outside the church, no salvation." The second extreme would minimize the necessity and universality of the church, as if to suggest that the church is the means of salvation intended only for its members.[23] Dupuis finds an alternative to these positions in the conciliar notion of being "oriented" to the church. *Lumen gentium* teaches that "those who have not yet received the gospel are ordained, in various ways, to the People of God" (no. 16). John Paul II teaches that those who follow other religious paths can be saved by "a grace which, while having a mysterious relationship to the church, does not make them formally part of the church but enlightens them in a way which is accommodated to their spiritual and material situation" (*RM*, no. 10). In Dupuis's view, instead of "belonging" to the church, Hindus, Buddhists, Muslims, and others are "oriented" toward the church as the fullness of the means of salvation.[24]

PLURALIST THEOLOGIES

In fulfillment theologies the various religious traditions find their ultimate meaning in Christ. The salvation these religions provide is always the work of the Holy Spirit revealing Jesus Christ, the one great mediation of God and creation. Thus the universal religious quest for God leads to the historical person of Jesus and his followers, the church. Some Catholic theologians have begun to ask if God's salvation is available apart from Christ and the church. In contrast to the fulfillment model, this approach may loosely be called a pluralist theology of religions.

Pluralist theologies of religions are often indebted to John Hick's philosophy of religion.[25] As a response to religious diversity, Hick argues, Christians and others should adopt the hypothesis that "the great world traditions constitute different conceptions and perceptions of, and responses to, the Real from within the different cultural ways of being human."[26] Religious terms for an impersonal Ultimate Reality, like Brahman, Sunyata, and the Dao, as well as for personal deities such as Allah, Yahweh, Shiva, Amaterasu, and Kali are different ways human beings have of naming and connecting with what Hick calls the Real. As a consequence, all religions must be seen as partial and incomplete interpretations of a transcendent Reality that utterly surpasses our ability to comprehend. No religion may legitimately claim to be superior to any other religion as a path to salvation. This means that Hick does not define the term *salvation* as it is understood in fulfillment theologies. For Hick, salvation is more than communion with the Holy Trinity in the kingdom of God. In order to include all the religions, Hick understands salvation very generically as a shift from "ego-centeredness" to "Reality-centeredness."

Hick's approach to religious diversity has been criticized in more than one official document of the Catholic Church as a form of religious relativism.[27] Being a Muslim or a Buddhist, a Zoroastrian or a Christian is largely an accident of birth and always a matter of legitimate choice, in Hick's view. Changing from one religion to another may reflect personal taste or psychological aptitude. Conversion to one particular religion, however, is not necessary for salvation. All religions provide more or less equal access to Reality-centeredness.

The pluralist approach to the diversity of religions brings with it implications for Christian belief, especially Christianity's understanding of Jesus Christ as the unique and universal savior of the world.[28] To date, the most sophisticated attempt to think about Jesus Christ in light of the pluralist view of religions can be found in the work of Roger Haight, SJ.[29] The appeal to a "Spirit-christology," which is at the center of Haight's proposal, is too complicated by far to be treated here. Haight asks, "Is Christianity really a religion destined for all people?" The answer Haight gives "leans on the side of pluralism."[30] Christians must believe that Jesus is a normative revelation from God, but they may also believe that God is normatively revealed in other religious traditions as well. In this, Haight's goal is to understand Jesus Christ as *one* savior among others, recognizing that faith in Jesus Christ may not be the only way to salvation. Haight wants to contribute to a "pluralist theology" that reflects a "global consciousness" and resists the "sectarian temptation" that has led to Christianity's claim that faith in Jesus Christ is the only way God's salvation is available to human beings.[31]

In Haight's Spirit-christology, Jesus of Nazareth is the way God's saving Spirit is present in the world for Christians. Jesus Christ is therefore the paramount religious truth within the Christian tradition but not within the other paths. Haight does not mean to imply that other religious leaders, like Muhammad and Confucius, should necessarily be thought of as incarnations of God, as in Christian belief. In other religions God's salvation can be mediated in various ways. Presumably, these mediations would include historical persons, like Zoroaster, and sacred texts, like the Qur'an, and even religious doctrines, like the Buddha's Four Noble Truths.[32]

In addition, Haight's pluralist theology of religions requires Christians to recognize that Jesus Christ is not the full revelation of God to the world. God is always more. Christians need to pay attention to other religious traditions in order to learn more of God:

Neither Jesus nor Christianity mediates any complete possession of God. Without a sense of God's transcendent mystery, without the healthy agnostic sense of what we do not know of God, one will not expect to learn more of God from what has been communicated to us human beings through other revelations and religions.[33]

The incompleteness of God's revelation in Jesus, however, does not make this revelation less true. Despite his incompleteness, Jesus remains the saving revelation of God for Christians, "the one who mediates God's salvation to humankind."[34] But Jesus is not the savior of people who follow other religious paths. For this reason, Jesus of Nazareth cannot be called a universal savior, the unique and unparalleled redemptive savior intended for all:

> The key step or point of transition to the pluralist position is the breakdown of a causal connection between Jesus of Nazareth, who is the basis of christology, and the salvation that according to Christian faith goes on outside of the Christian sphere.[35]

God's saving power is at work within each religious tradition in its own way. With Rahner, Haight argues that Sikhs and Muslims are saved by means of their own religious practices. Contrary to Rahner, Haight does not claim that Christ is at work in these religious practices. Sikhism and Islam are saving religions in their own right, apart from Christ. There are many separate paths that lead to one common salvation in God. Christ is the presence of God on earth for Christians. The Qur'an is the presence of God on earth for Muslims. The *dharma*, apparently, is God's earthly presence for Buddhists.

The basis for this assessment of other religious traditions lies in Haight's Spirit-christology. *Logos*-christologies, taking their cue from the Prologue of John's Gospel, think of salvation in terms of an "incarnation" of God as a human being: the Word *(Logos)* becomes flesh in the person of Jesus of Nazareth. *Logos*-christologies tend to reinforce the belief that Jesus Christ is the one and only incarnation that is the center of history and the sole source of salvation for the whole world. A Spirit-christology, in contrast, understands the divinity of Jesus in terms of the activity of the Spirit who has elected to dwell within him. The Spirit has descended on Jesus of Nazareth and raised him up as savior of the world. But the Spirit blows where the Spirit wills and descends on whomever and whatever the Spirit decides. Jesus, therefore, is not necessarily the only mediation of the Divine empowered by the Holy Spirit. A Spirit-christology prepares Christians to recognize other mediations of the saving power of God's Spirit better than a *Logos*-christology.

How does a Spirit-christology contribute to a pluralist theology of religions? Through the working of the Holy Spirit, Jesus of Nazareth has been empowered to save all. But Christians must recognize that the Spirit has been at work in the world from the beginning, "without a causal connection to the historical appearance of Jesus."[36] Therefore, by recognizing that the Spirit is not restricted to the confines of the Christian community, a Spirit-christology is capable of recognizing other mediations of God. "The Spirit is spread abroad and it is not necessary to think that God as Spirit can be incarnated only once in history."[37] In fact, the other religious traditions may be rooted in incarnations that are independent of the Christ event that forms the core of Christianity.

FAITHFUL TO THE TRADITION?

In his encyclicals John Paul II has developed a carefully crafted development of the council's vision of the other religious paths. Theologians like Jacques Dupuis and Roger Haight, in varying degrees, want to push further our appreciation of other religious paths as works of the Holy Spirit and as witnesses to the kingdom of God. How shall we evaluate this theological ferment? I propose two criteria. First, a theology of religions must be faithful to the depth and scope of Christian tradition. Second, a theology of religions must also be helpful to Christians today as they seek new forms of social and religious solidarity with other believers.

The first of the two criteria needs no justification. Christian tradition confronts us with two demanding truths: the uniqueness of Christ as savior of all and the universality of saving grace in the Holy Spirit. Any theological understanding of other religious traditions must be faithful to both of these doctrines. Anything less is inadequate to the scriptural witness and the richness of the tradition. Roman Catholic fulfillment theology can be evaluated against the first of the two criteria by contrasting it with other Christian approaches to religious diversity.

First, the fulfillment approach can be contrasted with what Paul Knitter calls the "replacement model" of the theology of religions embraced by many Evangelical Christians.[38] Replacement theologies, more often called exclusivist theologies, strongly emphasize the need to turn away from sinful ways and embrace the gospel by converting to Christianity. Other religious traditions are of little, if any, value. An Evangelical theologian like Karl Barth even argues that the religions are forms of "unbelief," because they are in "rebellion" against God revealed in Jesus Christ.[39] The doctrine "no salvation outside the church," even when tempered by the notion of baptism by desire, is a replacement theology. Salvation can be found only in Christianity, and in the stricter formulations, only in the Roman Catholic Church. Anything outside the ark of Peter is damned. The Christian religion, therefore, is intended by God to replace all the other religions.

Replacement theologies, Catholic or Protestant, fail to do justice to the many voices of the New Testament in regard to the meaning and status of other religious paths. To be sure, the Christian scriptures proclaim that there is "no other name" save that of Jesus Christ by which we are saved. But the Christian scriptures also testify to the universality of God's grace and the work of the Holy Spirit outside the confines of the Christian community. For this reason replacement theologies cannot be said to measure up to the first of the two criteria for evaluating a Christian theology of religions. These theologies are not faithful to the depth and scope of the tradition. In the Second Vatican Council, the Roman Catholic Church declined to speak of the other religious paths using the traditional formula "outside the church, no salvation." In doing so the council turned away from the replacement model of religious diversity. In embracing a fulfillment model the council was, in effect, expressing its desire to do justice not only to the uniqueness of Jesus Christ but also to the universality of grace in the work of the Holy Spirit. The movement from "outside the church" through the council to John Paul's theology of the Holy Spirit must be seen as a movement toward greater fidelity to the demands of Christian tradition.

Second, Roman Catholic fulfillment theology can be contrasted with what is often called the pluralist model of the theology of religions championed by John Hick. In his philosophy of religion Hick argues that we should assume that all religions are roughly equal attempts to interpret a transcendent Absolute, "the Real," that ultimately remains beyond our ability to express in language. Salvation is a matter of moving from ego-centeredness to Reality-centeredness. As no religion can claim to be any better than any other religion in its attempt to name the Ultimate, so also, no religion can claim to be superior to any other religion in providing a path that leads to salvation. Christians talk about faith in Jesus Christ. Hindus seek mystical union with Brahman. Buddhists meditate in order to achieve nirvana. Daoists talk about harmony with the Dao. Muslims call for submission to Allah. According to the pluralist model all these believers are really trying to name the same unnameable Ultimate Reality. There is nothing that is superior or unique in any religion, including Christianity and its faith in Jesus Christ.

Like replacement theologies, theologies based on the pluralist model fail to do justice to the demands of Christian tradition. If replacement theologies do not sufficiently honor the universality of God's grace and the unrestrained work of the Holy Spirit among all the religions, the pluralist model does not sufficiently honor the uniqueness of Jesus Christ. Christianity does not teach that Jesus is but one way among others to become "Reality-centered," as John Hick has argued. Instead, Jesus Christ is "the way, the truth, and the life." The Christ event is the one great mediation of grace that reconciles God and creation. All salvation is in Christ. The Second Vatican Council, in rejecting the older replacement theology, did not embrace the pluralist model. Instead, the council adopted a fulfillment approach. Religions are not roughly equal ways to reach the same salvation. Those who follow other religious paths can be saved. They can be saved by following the teachings and practices of their own religious traditions. But these religions are salvific only to the extent that they participate in the great mediation of grace that is Jesus Christ. Once again, fulfillment theologies succeed where other approaches fail. The pluralist model fails to honor Christian belief in the uniqueness of Jesus Christ as savior of all.

Currently, the most refined attempt to develop a theology of religions in the pluralist mold is the work of Roger Haight and his Spirit-christology. Christians must believe that Jesus is a normative revelation from God, but they must also believe that God is normatively revealed in the other paths as well. Jesus Christ is not the cause of the salvation of those who follow other religious paths.[40] Each religion has its own mediation of God that is salvific in its own right.

Haight's motivation in developing a Spirit-christology is, in part, to provide the basis for a pluralist theology of religions. This being the case, how does Haight's proposal measure up to the demands of the Christian tradition? Vatican documents have criticized the pluralist model as a form of religious relativism.[41] Haight's Spirit-christology, however, does not correspond very closely with Hick's philosophy of religion. In Hick's proposal, religions are human attempts at interpreting a transcendent Absolute that ultimately remains unknowable and unrevealed. For Haight, in contrast, the religions are all revelations from God, the work of the Holy Spirit witnessed to in Christianity. For Hick, the various religious paths should be seen as roughly equal ways to reach "Reality-centeredness," because, ultimately, it remains withdrawn from human history. For Haight, in contrast, the various religions are the result of multiple descents of the Holy Spirit into history. They are acts of God, historical revelations from God, not merely human attempts to interpret what remains unknowable. In addition, as a philosopher of religion Hick must posit a hypothetical metaphysical universal, the Real, which is common to all religions, no matter what theological language religious believers might actually use within their own traditions. The Real is a broader and more encompassing term than Allah, Brahman, Kali, and the Dao. The Real is broader than what Haight means when he speaks of God, and certainly broader than the Holy Spirit of Christian faith. If Hick sets the standard, Haight is not a very good pluralist. Muslims and Hindus might recognize what Haight means by *God*. Daoists and Buddhists would not. Haight's dissatisfaction with Hick's Christology, therefore, should come as no surprise.[42] For Hick, Jesus is a very charismatic man. The doctrine of the incarnation is a myth or non-literal way of talking about the Real. Other religious traditions have their own ways of talking about the Real. Haight's strong sense of Christian revelation will not let him adopt this philosophical position. For Haight, Jesus is "empowered" by the Holy Spirit in a positive act of God working within human history. In fact, there are other empowerments by the Holy Spirit within the other religions as well. If Haight finds Hick's christology "too thin,"[43] presumably, Hick would look on Haight's entire approach to religious diversity as too Christian.

Haight's Spirit-christology also needs to be compared with the theology of the Holy Spirit as articulated in the encyclicals of John Paul II. Roger Haight and the pope both are keen to recognize the work of the Holy Spirit within the various religious traditions. The pope's fulfillment approach, however, always links the work of the Spirit in the other religious paths to Christianity's faith in Jesus Christ. There is no economy of the Holy Spirit apart from the incarnation of the Word. Therefore, the work of the Holy Spirit in the multiple religious paths finds its ultimate meaning revealed in the Christ event to which Christianity bears full witness.

Unlike replacement theologies and pluralist theologies, fulfillment theologies succeed best in meeting the twin requirements of the Christian tradition. Jesus Christ is the unique savior of all, and at the same time, the grace of God is universal. Fidelity to the demands of Christian tradition, however, is but one criterion for evaluating a theology of religion. There remains yet another criterion against which any Christian understanding of other religions must be measured.

HELPFUL FOR TODAY?

The amount of violence motivated by religious fanaticism in the world today should be more than enough justification for the second of the two criteria. Any theological interpretation of the meaning and status of other religious traditions, in addition to being faithful to Christian tradition, must also be helpful to the Christian community today as it seeks new forms of social and religious solidarity with those who follow other religious paths. Religiously motivated violence, however, is by no means the only reason for the second criterion. Diana Eck, director of the Pluralism Project at Harvard University, has written that the United States is the most religiously pluralistic nation in the world.[44] The notion of America as a Judeo-Christian nation, let alone a Christian commonwealth, falls far short of the mark in describing the religious ethos of the United States. Moreover, to the consternation of the secularization theorists, the United States is one of the most religiously observant countries in the world. American Christians have a responsibility to promote new forms of social and religious solidarity that reach beyond the "old diversity" of Catholics, Protestants, and Jews.

Africa is a place where Christians and Muslims will have to find ways of living together. The same can be said of Europe. In India, Hindu nationalists have rejected the secular vision of Nehru. In the face of violence against many religious communities in India, including the Christian minority, Indian Christians need to build new forms of solidarity with Dalits, Tribals, Sikhs, Jains, Parsis, Muslims, and of course, Hindus. As Roman Catholic thinking about other religious traditions has developed over the last fifty years, the world has become more complex and interdependent. The need for new forms of social and religious solidarity has increased, not decreased. How, then, does Roman Catholic fulfillment theology measure up to the second of the two criteria?

Fulfillment theologies are not adequate to the needs of the Christian community today. They are not helpful, or at least not helpful enough, to Christians as they seek ways to live creatively and responsibly with their neighbors who follow other religious paths. The development of a fulfillment theology of religions over the last fifty years constitutes a significant achievement for Christian faith. The work of theologians like Daniélou and Rahner, the documents of the Second Vatican Council, and the efforts of Pope John Paul II were instrumental in bringing the Catholic Church out of a stance of hostility and fear toward other religions to an attitude of genuine tolerance and even respect. This period of innovation in the area of the theology of religions, I believe, is drawing to an end. A fulfillment model for understanding the status and meaning of other religious traditions, as we have seen, is the most faithful to the complex demands of Christian tradition. The development of a fulfillment theology over the last fifty years has been a necessary and welcome step for Roman Catholics. But faithful as it is to Christian tradition, I do not believe that fulfillment theology will adequately serve the Christian community in the new century.

Claiming that the fulfillment model is inadequate to the needs of the Christian community today, despite its fidelity to the demands of Christian tradition, is a considerable criticism. In making my point, I want to highlight the following problems: (1) continuing the debate over a theology of religions amounts to Christians talking to themselves; (2) fulfillment theologies distort other religious traditions; (3) the fulfillment model minimizes the significance of religious differences; and (4) the fulfillment model is not helpful in promoting effective interreligious dialogue.

TALKING TO OURSELVES

In the debate over a proper theology of religions during the last fifty years, we have been talking to ourselves. This intra-Christian conversation has been necessary. Now, given the pressing need for new forms of social and religious solidarity among religious communities, Christians need to start talking to those who follow other religious paths.

Of its very nature a theology of religions entails a conversation in which Christians talk with other Christians. Other religious communities, of course, have their own theologies of religions, and the same holds true for these theologies as well. In the Christian discussion this can be seen in the fact that the debate has focused almost completely on the issue of whether other religious believers can be saved. The number of questions asked is severely limited. Can those who follow other religious paths be saved by Christ? If so, are they saved despite their specific religious practices or because of them? The council, for example, moved decisively beyond the principle of "outside the church, no salvation" to affirm unambiguously that other religious believers can be saved by Christ. John Paul II went further to say that Christ saves Muslims and Hindus, Confucians and Daoists, Buddhists and animists by means of their religious practices, not in spite of them. The problem with this limited set of questions is that it yields a limited set of answers. Fulfillment theologies ask a Christian question of the Christian tradition and end up with a Christian answer. What does Christian tradition say about those who follow other religious paths? They can be saved, by Christ and the Holy Spirit acting through these other religious traditions. Absent from the conversation are the voices of those who are being discussed. The fact that the entire discussion of the salvation of others is often unintelligible or even offensive to other religious believers is never allowed to enter into the theological discussion. The conversation remains safely confined to Christians talking to Christians— calls for interreligious dialogue notwithstanding. At what point does Christian fulfillment theology have the unintended effect of silencing other religious believers? At what point does the restricting of the conversation to Christians become a way of excusing ourselves from the obligation to listen to and learn from other religious believers?

Let me offer an example. The Venerable Karuna Dharma, a Buddhist nun in a Vietnamese lineage, recalls speaking to an audience of Christians about the dynamic interaction of meditation and compassionate action in her tradition. The Christians, she lamented, learned very little about Buddhism on that occasion because they kept assuring her that meditation and compassion are really linked by the Holy Spirit working within Buddhists. This Buddhist nun knows well that Buddhists and Christians have their own ways of talking about religious matters, including the religious practices of others. However, when our need to explain Buddhism begins to interfere with our ability to listen to Buddhists, our explanations may be compliant with the demands of Christian faith, but they are no longer very helpful. Fulfillment theologies offer a very plausible explanation of other religious traditions, plausible, at least, for Christians. Of all the possible candidates for a theology of religions, a fulfillment theology is by far the most faithful to the richness of Christian tradition. This approach, however, fails to be very helpful to Christians who, today especially, need to find ways to relate themselves in creative new ways to those who follow other religious paths. The more we focus on developing this kind of theology, the more we continue to talk to ourselves. For fifty years this conversation has been helpful to Roman Catholics. This is no longer the case.

DISTORTING OTHER RELIGIONS FOR CHRISTIAN PURPOSES

Another reason that fulfillment theologies fail to measure up to the second criterion is that they distort the teachings of other religious traditions. This puts Christians in the unhelpful position of claiming to know more about the religious lives of other believers than they know about themselves. Moreover, fulfillment theologies place Christians in this unhelpful position because they try to solve problems endemic to Christianity, not the other religions. Christians need to find better solutions to their own theological and pastoral problems

First, fulfillment theologies require Christians to make statements about other religious believers that those "others" find puzzling, mistaken, or even offensive. For example, fulfillment theologies suggest that Christians should recognize in Theravada Buddhism the action of the Holy Spirit within history. Of course, the universality of God's grace transforming all of creation is a great Christian truth. At the same time, this statement entails a significant distortion of Buddhism. Theravada Buddhists do not believe in God. They do not believe in a Holy Spirit active within history. Even more fundamentally, they do not believe that there is any such thing as history, at least history as it is understood by Christians as God's unfolding eschatological plan. Understanding what is strange in terms of what is familiar is basic to any act of understanding. Imposing what is known on that which is unknown in a way that distorts the unknown, however, cannot be called an act of understanding in any proper sense of the word.

Second, Christians who make such statements about other religious believers are motivated, at least in part, by the need to solve problems within Christianity. The principle of "outside the church, no salvation" is neither plausible nor acceptable to most people today, including most Christians. For many Christians the idea of baptism by desire *(in voto)* seems like casuistry of the most self-serving sort. Fulfillment theology helps contemporary Christians to deal with a sizable credibility problem. The vast majority of human beings who have ever lived are not damned by the "good news" of Christianity. Other religious believers can be saved just as Christians are saved: by the grace of the Holy Spirit. Here again, the relationship between the two criteria is apparent. In regard to the first criterion, the fulfillment approach is the most consistent with Christian tradition. Faithful to the tradition though it is, however, fulfillment theologies also lead Christians to make statements about other religious paths that wildly distort their teachings. This is done in order to fix a problem inherent within Christianity; that is, how could a benevolent God condemn the vast majority of human beings now alive to perdition because they are not explicitly members of the Christian community?

During the Second Vatican Council the document on the other religious traditions, *Nostra aetate (NA),* was being worked out at the same time as the document on religious freedom, *Dignitatis humanae (DH).* "Error has its rights" was a catch phrase during the debate on the document on religious freedom. This position would be easier to accept if the other religions could be said to "reflect a ray of that truth which enlightens all men," as the final text of *Nostra aetate* assures. The Catholic Church was able to adopt a position of tolerance of other religions, in part, by shifting from a replacement theology to a fulfillment theology. However historic these Council documents may be, today Christians need to ask if other religions are tolerable only after their teachings have been significantly distorted to conform to Christian expectations. "Tolerance" of this kind does not serve Christians very well today. Hinduism should be tolerated by Christians not because it is merely a paler version of Christian faith but because it is different. In fact, the new forms of social and religious solidarity called for by the gospel today will require Christians to go far beyond toleration, virtuous as it may be, to esteem other religious believers because of the significant differences that separate them from the Christian community.

DOMESTICATING DIFFERENCES

In addition to distorting the other religions, fulfillment theologies fail to measure up to the demands of the second criterion in yet another way. Despite their good intentions, fulfillment theologies imply that other religious traditions are of no value to the extent that they are different from Christianity. What is "true and holy" in the other religions is what is already familiar to Christians. Buddhism and Islam, Confucianism and Jainism are to be respected and taken seriously because, despite what they might say about themselves, they are actually the result of the working of the Holy Spirit. Of course, other religious traditions are very different from Christianity in much of their teachings and practices. From a fulfillment perspective, these differences are in some cases tolerable and in other cases lamentable. Religious differences, however, are never of genuine religious value or theological interest to Christians. What is of value in other religious traditions are the truths Christians know already. This state of affairs needs to be seen as a momentous loss for Christians today. Fulfillment theologies hobble Christians in their attempt to engage other religious believers in new and creative ways. In this respect they do not measure up to the second of the two criteria for a suitable understanding of other religions.

Buddhism, as we will see in the chapters to come, teaches truths that are at times profoundly different from the truths known to Christians. Sometimes the unfamiliar truths of Buddhism are deeply illuminating for Christians. At other times the teachings of Buddhism are puzzling, disconcerting, or implausible to Christians. No matter how strange, no matter how different, fulfillment theologies keep the strangeness of Buddhism safely under control. For all its strangeness, Buddhism is really a more obscure version of what is already familiar to Christians. The strangeness of Buddhism, therefore, poses no danger to Christian faith. The teachings of Buddhism, at least the teachings that are true and holy, are the work of the Holy Spirit. Despite the significant ways in which it differs from Christianity, the strangeness of Buddhism will never require Christians to think in new ways about their own tradition.

Fulfillment theologies, therefore, have the unwelcome effect of cutting Christians off from the transformative power of the other religious traditions and their unfamiliar teachings. This must be counted as a lost opportunity for Christians in two ways. First, it is a lost opportunity for developing new forms of social and religious solidarity among Christians and the other religious communities. Second, it is a lost opportunity for enriching Christian faith by learning from the strangeness of the other religious traditions. Christians need to relate to those who follow the other paths in a way that not only tolerates differences but actually is eager to learn from differences. This openness to learning should be recognized as a new form of religious solidarity between religious communities. The strangeness of the other religions is not something to be avoided or merely tolerated because we "know" in advance that, despite what other believers say about themselves, they are really being shaped by the Holy Spirit.

John Paul II's theology of the Holy Spirit, as we have seen, is a skillful development of the generally positive vision of the other religions found in the documents of the Second Vatican Council. The pope's teaching accounts for religious differences in terms of the principle of "participated forms of mediation" (*RM*, no. 5). This means that other religious traditions are salvific to the degree that they mediate the saving grace of Christ by participating in the universal and normative mediation of grace that is Christ and Christ's church. This also means that Christians should expect to find hidden within other religious traditions the same saving grace that they find in their own community. Where other religions are different or strange, Christians should press on to discover what is familiar. The principle of a participated mediation, although it is a genuine contribution to Christian tradition that reflects the complexity that has gone before it, is not very helpful in empowering Christians to open their minds to the strangeness and "otherness" of those who follow the other religious paths. In the fulfillment paradigm difference has been safely domesticated. Differences are a matter of error or mere human achievement. Where Christians find religions recognizable and familiar, they may affirm that these religions participate in the mediation of grace that is Christ and the church.

By making the teachings and practices of other religious traditions less of a threat to Christian faith, fulfillment theologies also render these religions less interesting. For example, seen from the perspective of a fulfillment theology, the Buddhist understanding of compassion through the practice of selflessness presents no serious challenge to Christian faith. Buddhist compassion can be embraced by Christians as a sign of the Holy Spirit because it is analogous to Christian love. However, Buddhists also teach that human beings should renounce their belief in God as an unhelpful entanglement that does not lead to liberation from suffering. This teaching may be puzzling to Christians. Some Christians may look on this teaching as "error" that "has its rights." The fulfillment approach, however, never asks Christians to look on this significant religious difference as theologically interesting. Fulfillment theologies alert Christians to be interested in similarities, not differences. For example, Muslims are similar to Christians in their affirmation of the existence of one God. For a fulfillment theology, this is significant. Muslims also look on Jesus as a prophet, like Muhammad, not a savior, and certainly not the incarnate Son of God. But for fulfillment theologies, this difference is neither theologically interesting nor religiously challenging. From within the fulfillment framework, Islam's radical monotheism fails to provide an opportunity for Christian theological reflection because it is never allowed to pose a threat to Christian belief. The significance of Islam is found in the fact that it is a participated form of mediation in which truths that are clearly visible in Christianity are discernable although obscured in Islam. The other religious traditions, each in its own way, bring with them teachings that pose enormous opportunities for Christians to think about themselves and their faith in new ways. Christians should look on this as an opportunity for self-enrichment and for forging new forms of social and religious solidarity today. Fulfillment theologies excuse Christians from having to grapple with this challenge. In this respect fulfillment theologies are not helpful to Christians today in finding new and creative ways of engaging religious diversity and building solidarity between religious communities.

THE IMPACT ON INTERRELIGIOUS DIALOGUE

The Second Vatican Council, with its fulfillment theology, is often remembered for its call to Christians to enter into dialogue with followers of other religious traditions (e.g., *NA*, no. 6; *AG*, nos. 52 and 59; *Gaudium et spes* [*GS*], no. 81). Even though the connection between the Roman Catholic Church's positive reevaluation of other religions and its newfound commitment to interreligious dialogue cannot be denied, the problems associated with the fulfillment theologies we have been discussing bring with them disconcerting implications for the practice of interreligious dialogue. Fulfillment theologies distort the teachings of other religious traditions for Christian purposes. They tend to domesticate religious differences by rendering them theologically uninteresting. Despite all the talk about the importance of interreligious dialogue associated with the debate over the theology of religions, the discussion itself has tended to marginalize dialogue by deferring it while Christians continue to talk to themselves. All of these problems associated with fulfillment theologies and the theology of religions more generally tend to make interreligious dialogue less urgent for Christians and less valuable.

Fulfillment theologies lessen the urgency for dialogue with other religious believers. If Christians can know in advance that what is "true and holy" in the religious lives of other religious believers will reveal what is already known to Christians, then dialogue with other religions cannot have the same urgency it otherwise would have. Fulfillment theologies allow some Christian theologians to think of themselves as having a positive and tolerant view of other religious believers and then to move on to less "exotic" issues within the Christian tradition. Since we already know in advance the theological meaning of these religions, we are excused from learning any more about them. Once we are excused from learning about other religious believers, we are excused from learning from them by meeting with them in dialogue.

Fulfillment theologies also undermine the value of interreligious dialogue. Since Christians can know in advance that, despite what Muslims and Buddhists, Jains and Hindus might say about themselves, what is good and true in other religious traditions is the work of the same Spirit that animates Christianity, the purpose and value of dialogue is undermined. No matter how different another religion may be, and no matter what religious believers may say about themselves during a dialogue meeting, Christians know in advance that what is being said is either irrelevant or merely a paler version of what Christians know already. The impact of this on dialogue is deadly. Dialogue becomes a tame and low-stakes affair, theologically safe and unchallenging. Dialogue has value as an exercise in ecclesial diplomacy, not theological inquiry. The importance of diplomatic relations among religious communities and institutions is not to be taken for granted. However, when dialogue with other religious believers is no longer significant as a mode of theological inquiry, the value of interreligious dialogue has been undermined. By undermining the theological value of dialogue, fulfillment theologies fail to measure up to the second of the two criteria. Fulfillment theologies are not helpful to Christians today who want to be engaged by other religious believers in new and theologically creative ways.

The notion of Christianity as a fulfillment of the religious aspiration of other religious believers can be seen in a statement made about interreligious dialogue in the *Catechism of the Catholic Church*. According to the *Catechism* the missionary task of the church includes a "respectful dialogue" with other religious believers in which Christians proclaim the good news "in order to consolidate, complete and raise up the truth and the goodness that God has distributed among men and nations, and to purify them from error and evil" (no. 856). Statements such as this are neither comforting nor encouraging to the Catholic Church's dialogue partners. The *Catechism's* view of dialogue, however, is very much the product of the official fulfillment theology. Never does the *Catechism* suggest that Christians have anything to learn from other religious traditions. If, theologically speaking, Christianity is the fulfillment of the other religions, linking dialogue with the fulfillment of the religious aspirations of the dialogue partner is not difficult. This linkage tends to obscure both the religious goals of other believers as well as their motivation for dialoguing with Christians to begin with. Should Christians presume that Jews engage in dialogue with Christians in order to find the fulfillment of their Jewish faith? Christians are often surprised when they hear that some Buddhists dialogue with Christians simply in order to promote a better understanding of their religion in predominantly Christian countries like the United States. These Buddhists have little expectation that Christianity has anything useful to teach them.

THE REGNOCENTRIC THEOLOGIANS

Given these problems with fulfillment theologies, we might ask about Jacques Dupuis and the regnocentric orientation of many Asian theologians. How helpful is this theology for Christians today? Dupuis's command of scripture, patristic tradition, Roman documents, and even Eastern Orthodox theology obscures the fact that his theology of religious diversity deeply reflects his sustained dialogue with Hindu thought and his many years of pastoral experience in India. Dupuis and Asian theologians like him are developing a truly *contextual* theology of religions. This Asian theology is to be rooted in the pastoral experiences of the Asian churches and yet is a theology that speaks to and challenges local churches around the world, including the local church of Rome.[45] Jacques Dupuis is a contextual theologian, and so, of course, am I. My own context as a theologian is dialogue with Buddhists (primarily Mahayana) in Japan and the United States, not with Hindus in India. This difference in context is significant. India and the United States are obviously different countries, religiously and in other ways. Moreover, in terms of the challenges they present to Christians, Hindus and Buddhists make very different dialogue partners.

For too many Catholic theologians, the fulfillment model has allowed interreligious dialogue to become something that is talked about more than practiced. This criticism does not apply to major Asian theologians. Jacques Dupuis, for example, insists that the starting point for a theology of religions is dialogue with other religious believers. Christian discourse about other religions is possible only after we have learned about them by dialoguing with them.[46]

The regnocentric approach, however, is still cast within the parameters of the theology of religions. As such, it shares to a degree in the problems associated with fulfillment theologies. Regnocentric theologies, for example, involve Christians in saying things about other religious believers that they do not say about themselves. This puts Christians in the unhappy position of claiming to know more about other religious believers than they know about themselves. For example, Jacques Dupuis writes,

> While believers of other religious faiths perceive God's call through their own traditions and respond to it in the sincere practice of these traditions, they become in all truth—even without being formally conscious of it— active members of the Kingdom.[47]

This statement confronts us with the great truth and the unavoidable weakness of a regnocentric theology of religions and, for that matter, of a fulfillment theology. On the one hand, the universal work of the Holy Spirit requires Christians to stand in silent respect before acts of community service, nonviolence, and compassion. How can such moral depth not be recognized as the work of the Spirit bringing about the kingdom? On the other hand, the other religions do not claim to be building up God's kingdom. To assert that this is what other religious believers are really doing, "even without being formally conscious of it," distorts the teaching of these religions.

For example, regnocentric Christians would presumably be eager to embrace Gandhi's "truth-struggle" *(satyagraha)* as a Hindu expression of kingdom-oriented, nonviolent activity. Likewise, these same Christians would find dialogue with Hindus of Vivekananda's community service movement congenial. But what about Hindus for whom "true Hinduism" is at variance with what these Christians consider to be paramount gospel values? Dialogue with Hindus who practice Gandhi's *satyagraha* is one thing. What about dialogue with a village Brahman who considers duties to caste and the social discrimination that flows from these duties to be at the heart of the Hindu religious worldview? Christians, from the perspective of their own religious tradition, are justified in praising *satyagraha* and rejecting caste discrimination. Christians are also justified in claiming, on Christian grounds, that Hindus who practice *satyagraha* are cooperating with the Holy Spirit in the building up of the kingdom. The regnocentric perspective, however, is not a very helpful way of understanding Hinduism on its own terms. Imposing this Christian perspective on Hinduism distorts this religious tradition.

Buddhism offers another example. The Dalai Lama speaks, with eloquence, about the importance of respecting human rights. The regnocentric perspective advises Christians to look at the Dalai Lama's efforts as yet another way in which the Holy Spirit is bringing about God's kingdom of justice and peace outside the confines of the Christian community. I am in agreement with regnocentric theologians like Jacques Dupuis and Michael Amaladoss that Christian tradition allows us to interpret the efforts of the Dalai Lama in this way. But what about the many Buddhists who do not see the assertion of human rights as compatible with Buddhism? The Venerable Dhammapidok, one of the most respected and learned Buddhist monks in Thailand, teaches that human rights are foreign to the Buddhist worldview. Venerable Dhammapidok is by no means a supporter of torture or the suppression of civic freedoms. The idea of individuals *asserting* their rights, however, is not compatible with the path of selflessness taught by the Buddha. For Dhammapidok, the assertion of human rights is yet another symptom of *samsara,* the realm of passion and suffering.[48] From a regnocentric perspective, the Buddhism that is to be esteemed is the Buddhism of the Dalai Lama. What is to be said of the Buddhism of the Venerable Dhammapidok? Should Christians pass over this Buddhism in silence or criticize it as contrary to Christian hope in the kingdom? The Venerable Dhammapidok has something to teach Christians that does not fit neatly into their established expectations about the kingdom of

God. Regnocentric theologies, and fulfillment theologies more generally, are not helpful to Christians in dealing with this fact.

Fulfillment theologies distort other religions by casting them as paler versions of what is seen more clearly and decisively in Christianity. This is unfortunately the case even with Jacques Dupuis's sophisticated view of the other religions. For example, Dupuis argues that the religious practices of other religions are "the visible element, the sign, the sacrament" of their experience of Christ, despite what other religious believers might say about themselves. Once these religions have been conformed to fit into a Christian mold, Dupuis is required to admit that they suffer in comparison:

> There is only one mystery of salvation in Christ. But this mystery is present to human beings outside the bounds of Christianity. In the church, an eschatological community, it is present to them openly and explicitly, in the full visibility of his complete mediation. In the other religious traditions, it is present hiddenly and implicitly, through a modality of incomplete, but no less real, mediation, constituted by such traditions.[49]

Christianity sets the agenda, then the other religious traditions are found praiseworthy but lacking in various ways. Even though the rites and practices of the other religions must be recognized as mediations of the mystery of Christ, these rites and practices are "not on the same level as the Christian sacraments and "incomplete and open to a fuller self-gift and disclosure on the part of God."[50]

At the heart of the matter is the fact that regnocentric theologies are a species of fulfillment theology and share in both the strengths and weaknesses of fulfillment theologies. As developed by the council and subsequently by John Paul II, those who follow other religious paths find the fulfillment of their religious aspirations in Christ. Although the church cannot simply be identified with the kingdom of God, neither can the church be completely separated from it. Regnocentric theologies seek to minimize the role of the church by asserting that Christianity joins all the other religious traditions in finding its own fulfillment in the kingdom of God. The regnocentric model, to the extent that it does not completely separate the church from the kingdom of God, is in conformity with conciliar and papal teaching. In regard to the second criterion, Asian theologians have been creative in the quest for new forms of social and religious solidarity. However, no matter how committed to solidarity with other religious believers regnocentric theologians may be, the regnocentric approach is not free of problems in regard to the second of the two criteria for evaluating a Christian understanding of other religious traditions.

SPIRIT-CHRISTOLOGY

Does the Spirit-christology being developed by Roger Haight provide an alternative to fulfillment theologies? Many of Haight's critics have focused on issues associated with the first of the two criteria for evaluating any Christian understanding of other religious traditions, that is, fidelity to the demands of Christian tradition. What about the second of the two criteria? Is a Spirit-christology helpful to the Christian community today?

A Spirit-christology would lead us to expect that the Holy Spirit is visibly at work within Buddhism, just as the Spirit is at work within Christianity. In fact, this approach permits us to believe that the Spirit has established a mediation of the Divine within Buddhism as the Spirit has done in Christ for Christianity. What might a Buddhist mediation of the Divine look like? The Buddha? The *dharma*? In the case of Pure Land Buddhism, Christians should presumably look on Amida Buddha as a mediation of the Divine brought about by the power of the Holy Spirit. I explained this view to a group of Pure Land Buddhists in Japan. Their response was twofold. First, they noted that to understand what is strange (Amida) in terms of what is familiar (Christ) is only natural. Their second response was to ask how Buddhists might help Christians get over this misunderstanding of the Pure Land path. Amida Buddha is not a god, and certainly not God. A Spirit-christology makes this task all the more daunting, in part because it has been developed to respond to Christianity's problem with credibility, not to engage Buddhists.

As with the official fulfillment theology, Haight's Spirit-christology must distort the teachings of other religious traditions in order to fix problems plaguing Christianity. Haight's approach, however, does not distort all religions equally. Vaishnavite Hinduism, which is centered on devotion to Lord Vishnu and his multiple *avatars* ("divine descents"), might find Haight's understanding of the descent of the Holy Spirit into the world more congenial than Pure Land Buddhists. In fact, some Vaishnavite Hindus recognize the historical Buddha and Jesus of Nazareth as *avatars* of Lord Vishnu along with Krishna and Rama. Islam, however, would be another matter. Is Muhammad a mediation of God, equal to Jesus Christ in his power to save? Almost all Muslims will find this claim a distortion of their religion and very objectionable, if not blasphemous. Haight himself advises us that God is mediated within other religions is multiple ways.[51] If Muhammad is not a Spirit-empowered mediation of the Divine, then perhaps the Qur'an is. Some Muslims might find this more congenial to their faith, although their understanding of the Spirit would be very different than Roger Haight's. If God can be mediated by a book as well as a sacred person, should Christians look on the Heart Sutra as a divine mediation? This Buddhist text, with its famous phrase "form is emptiness and emptiness is form," erodes the very notion of a Creator-God as in Christian tradition. Claiming that the Heart Sutra is a mediation of God in the world imposes a religious worldview on the text that is very foreign to it.

In some forms of neo-Confucianism the emperor of China is recognized as the great mediator between heaven (*T'ien*) and earth. In order to be tolerant toward neo-Confucians and plausible in the eyes of the modern world, should Christians believe that Chinese emperors are divine mediations equal to Jesus Christ? In some forms of Shintoism today, the emperor of Japan is seen as a god (*kami*). Should the occupant of the Chrysanthemum throne also be seen as a human mediation of God equal to Christ? At the very least, Haight's proposal about the possibility of recognizing multiple mediations of the Divine outside of the Christian dispensation brings with it a demand for discernment. Clarifying what criteria would be appropriate for discerning a genuine mediation of the Divine in another religious tradition might be an illuminating exercise for Christians. Such an exercise, however, does nothing to address the concerns of the Pure Land Buddhists mentioned above. Spirit-christologies systematically distort the teachings of other religious traditions.

Moreover, the Spirit-christology approach also distorts Christian teaching in perhaps unforeseen ways. The claim that there are multiple mediations of the Divine at work in other religious traditions that are equivalent to the Christ event of Christianity is a significant departure from Christian tradition. But if there are mediations equal to Christ in other traditions, we might ask if there are other mediations equal to Christ, within Christianity as well. For example, is Mary, mother of Jesus and mother of God, a mediation of the Divine? A Spirit-christology gives considerable support to a theology of Mary as co-redemptrix. If Kali, Hinduism's ferocious mother, and Amaterasu, Shintoism's sun goddess, are candidates for normative revelations of the Divine, equal to the revelation in Christ, Mary would seem to be a likely candidate as well.

THE END OF AN ERA

I have proposed two criteria for evaluating Christianity's view of other religious paths. Theologies of religions must be faithful to the complexity and depth of the tradition. In addition, they must also be helpful to Christian believers today in their efforts to build new forms of social and religious solidarity in a world of considerable religious diversity. Roman Catholic fulfillment theologies comply with the first criterion. They fail to meet the needs of the Christian community in regard to the second criterion.

A fifty-year period of theological development has reached its logical conclusion in the fulfillment model. In the twenty-first century Christians need to find an alternative to the entire project of a theology of religions. Preoccupation with a comprehensive interpretation of the other religious paths is neither necessary nor advisable for Christians committed to developing new forms of social and religious solidarity with those who follow other religious paths. Instead of a theology that attempts to account comprehensively for the religious lives of those who follow the other paths, Christians should set for themselves a considerably more modest goal. This will entail a shift from theory to praxis.

Christians have poured a great deal of creativity into theory during the past fifty years. During this time the fulfillment model emerged as a comprehensive theological account of Christianity's "other": those who follow the other religious paths. There is in contemporary hermeneutics a great concern for the integrity of the "other" and resisting the tendency to render this "other" as "simply more of the same."[52] Christian theology needs to respond in greater depth to the contemporary turn away from hegemonic and homogenizing discourse like

Rahner's notion of a "universal religious experience" underlying all the religions. Especially, there is increased suspicion of grand narratives that purport to explain all and account for all from a perspective that remains unaffected by what is explained. Theologies of religions including those that measure up to the demands of the Christian tradition, are such grand narratives. This dissatisfaction with grand narratives poses a challenge to Christians. I also believe that it constitutes an opportunity for Christians.

DOING CHRISTIAN THEOLOGY WITH OTHERS

Now attention needs to be shifted from fulfillment theology as theory to interreligious dialogue as praxis. The purpose of this "doing before knowing" is not to overturn the achievement of the fulfillment model. My constant position has been that this theology is the most faithful to the wealth of Christian tradition of all the candidates for a theology of religions. Rather, the purpose of the shift away from theory is to recognize that interreligious dialogue is a way for the Christian community to become more creatively related to the other religious communities. Relating Christianity to the other religions by means of praxis, instead of a comprehensive theory, means that Christians will have to cultivate relationships with other religious believers that are not governed in advance by the grand narrative of a fulfillment theology or any other candidate for a theology of religions. Out of these relationships will come new forms of religious and social solidarity. Prolonging the debate over the theology of religions will only delay the turn from theory to praxis.

The praxis of interreligious dialogue, while it is an alternative to theologies of religions, is not meant to eclipse theology more generally. In fact, I propose that interreligious dialogue be recognized as the praxis of what can be called a comparative theology—a Christian theology done by means of dialogue with those who follow other religious paths. Comparative theology is not a theory that provides a foundation for praxis. Rather, the theology being proposed here is a critical reflection on praxis in the light of Christian faith. There has been much discussion in the debate over the theology of religions of the need to find a theoretical "foundation" or "basis" for dialogue.[53] The problems attending theologies of religions make clear how dubious this project is. Instead of using theology as a theoretical basis for dialogue, I propose to let dialogue be the basis, or praxis, of doing theology. Doing theology in dialogue with the others is not an attempt to provide a foundation or rationale *for* dialogue. Rather, what is called for is a theology that arises *through* dialogue. This is not a theology about interreligious dialogue, or a theology that justifies dialogue, but rather Christian theology itself carried out in dialogue with those who follow other religious paths.[54]

Moreover, interreligious dialogue is not merely a first step to a return to the discussion of the theology of religions. The Christian community does not need another theology of religions. Christians should set this project aside, recognizing that a half-century of creativity in this area has firmly established the fulfillment model, the most suitable of all the alternatives. Instead, they should begin to think about carrying out the entire project of theology—Christian faith seeking a relatively more adequate self-understanding given the contemporary situation—by means of dialogues with those who follow other religious traditions. The theology being proposed is not to be thought of as a new subdiscipline within theological inquiry, like scripture studies, liturgy, Christology, and ecclesiology. Rather, it is the church's theology itself in all its themes arising as a critical reflection on the church's praxis. In the case of comparative theology, the praxis entailed is the Christian community's dialogue with the other religious paths.

Unlike a theology of religions, doing Christian theology comparatively does not hope to establish a comprehensive account, or grand narrative, based solely on Christian faith, in which Buddhism or Islam, Hinduism or Confucianism appear as mere examples of a truth more clearly visible in Christianity. Instead of erecting an encompassing theory, this theology proceeds by means of very limited acts of interpretation rooted in the praxis of dialogue. Instead of distorting the "other" by construing it within a grand narrative, Christian theologians encounter that other as a partner in a dialogue. By critically reflecting on this praxis, the other becomes a resource for Christians in thinking about their faith in new ways. In the process, the Christian community builds new forms of social and religious solidarity with other religious communities.

For example, the great Japanese Pure Land Buddhist teacher Shinran (1173–1263) is renowned for his understanding of enlightenment as *shinjin*, which is often translated into English as "faith."[55] A theology of religions asks: Is this Buddhist "faith" really the work of the Holy Spirit, despite what Shinran and contemporary Pure Land Buddhists might say about it? A theology rooted in the praxis of dialogue asks a different and more constructive question: How does Shinran's understanding of enlightenment as "faith" help Christians to think in new ways about their own religious lives? For Shinran, *shinjin* does not imply belief in a savior God. Neither is there a notion of a "Spirit" in this Buddhist teaching. Moreover, there is no need for Christians to impose this Christian view on Buddhism. Instead, by means of dialogue with Pure Land Buddhists, Christians may discover both similarities and differences that are theologically challenging. By reflecting on the praxis of dialogue with these Buddhists, Shinran's teaching becomes a theological resource for Christians for renewing and deepening their own understanding of faith. In the process, Buddhists and Christians in Japan will have become related in new forms of social and religious solidarity.

In relation to Islam, theologies of religions are interested in whether Muhammad was inspired by the Holy Spirit in writing the Qur'an. Fulfillment theologies would tend to support this view without ever asking if Muslims think of Muhammad as the Qur'an's author. According to Muslim teaching, the Qur'an has no human author. The text was "recited" by Muhammad in response to a message from Allah dictated by the archangel Jabril (Gabriel). Doing theology in dialogue with Muslims, on the other hand, suggests a more helpful question: How does the Islamic understanding of the Qur'an as "recitation" enable Christians to think in new ways about the theology of revelation? Muslims look on Muhammad's recitation as perfect and free of any human additions to God's message. In contrast, God's revelation to the Jews (Torah) and to the Christians (the New Testament) are polluted with merely human fabrications *(shirk)* that do not come from God. The perfect revelation of the Qur'an fulfills and perfects the first two attempts at revelation. The revelation of God in the Qur'an is the final revelation, and Muhammad is the seal of the prophets. This Islamic fulfillment theology provides a genuine opportunity for Christians to think in new ways about their relationship with Jews. Has God's "new and eternal covenant" in Jesus abolished the covenant with the Jews? In recent years Roman Catholics have stopped saying this officially. In fact, some Vatican officials have claimed that the Catholic Church has no mission to evangelize the Jews.[56] Is this stance toward Jews compatible with the official fulfillment theology? Does fulfillment theology contain an implicit theology of abrogation? Doing Christian theology in dialogue with Muslims may have the unforeseen effect of establishing new forms of social and religious solidarity not only with Muslims but with Jews as well. This process begins only after Christians put aside their fulfillment theology of Islam and begin to take Islamic teaching seriously on its own terms.

A theology of religions approach would ask if the Jain practice of nonviolence *(ahimsa)* is really a sign that Jains are heirs to the kingdom of God proclaimed by Christ and realized in Christ's death and resurrection. Doing Christian theology in dialogue with Jains might ask a more theologically challenging question. In carefully controlled situations Jains sometimes express their religious vision of nonviolence by means of their ritual of voluntary death by starvation *(sallekhana)*. How might this ritual allow Christians to think in new ways about Christ's voluntary death on the cross? In light of this Jain ritual, how is Christ's voluntary death an overcoming of violence? Doing theology in dialogue with Jains does not deny what fulfillment theologies assert, that is, that Jains, especially in their practice of nonviolence, are heirs to the kingdom of God. However, it does not begin by asserting something about Jains that Jains do not claim about themselves. Instead, it begins with what Jains do say about themselves and tries to think about this as a possible resource for thinking in new ways about the meaning of Christian faith. Doing theology in dialogue with Jains may enable Christians to bring together some important themes in Christian theology in new ways. The theology of the cross, the renunciation of violence, and the coming of the kingdom of God may be related in ways that only Jains can teach us. Learning from Jains is yet another way for Christians to establish new forms of social and religious solidarity.

Christians have much to learn, positively and negatively, by recognizing that the fifty-year development of the theology of religions has reached a logical conclusion. Instead of trying to promote grand narratives about the others, we should begin to look on the teachings and practices of other religious traditions as resources for enriching Christian self-understanding. In the process, Christians and those who follow the other paths will enrich the world by forging bonds of respect and friendship. Doing Christian theology in dialogue with the other religions is a better way to respond creatively to the fact of religious diversity.

The chapters that follow offer an example of doing theology in dialogue with another religious tradition. A Christian text will be interpreted using a Buddhist text. Thomas Aquinas (1225–74), in his *Commentary on John*, talks about God as revealed in John's Gospel. In particular, Aquinas tries to think in some detail what it means to say that God is incomprehensible to the human mind. In his *Stanzas on the Middle Path*, the Buddhist thinker Nagarjuna (c. AD 150) develops a classic interpretation of the Buddhist doctrine of emptiness. The theological reflection that follows does not ask if Nagarjuna was inspired by the Holy Spirit. It does not begin with the presumption that Buddhist emptiness is a mediation of the Divine on a par with Jesus Christ. Rather, it seeks to understand the Buddhist text on its own terms, and then, based on this understanding, to ask if this Buddhist text might be a resource for Christians who seek to understand their own tradition in new ways. Aquinas (the familiar) will be read using Nagarjuna (the unfamiliar) in the hope of mining new insights about God from the quarry of this medieval Christian text. How will Nagarjuna, the Buddhist, allow us to understand Aquinas, the Christian, in new ways? This is but a small example of a larger project. More broadly, I hope to demonstrate that a serious study of Buddhism will reveal both intriguing similarities and puzzling differences when compared with Christianity. There will be no effort to overcome these differences or to interpret the similarities along the lines of a theology of religions. Instead, I hope to discuss Nagarjuna in light of what my Buddhist friends and teachers have taught me about Buddhist emptiness and to show that in learning about Nagarjuna and emptiness from Buddhists in dialogue, Christianity and Buddhism can become related in new and creative ways.

Before we can think in new ways about Aquinas using Nagarjuna as a resource, we have to understand Nagarjuna as a Buddhist teacher on his own terms, quite apart from what a Christian theology of religions might conclude about him. This means studying some of the basic teachings of Buddhism that Nagarjuna takes for granted. Chapter 2 has to do with these teachings attributed by Buddhists to Siddhartha Gautama, the historical Buddha. This chapter is by no means an introduction to Buddhism. The presentation should suffice to provide a context for Nagarjuna. Chapter 3 is a more specific discussion of Nagarjuna's *Stanzas on the Middle Path*. In effect, these two chapters amount to an initial dialogue with Buddhism. Chapter 4 uses Nagarjuna's notion of Buddhist emptiness to think about Aquinas's understanding of God. The last chapter is a reflection on this exercise in doing theology in dialogue with Buddhism.

2

A Man of Momentous Silence

In 1966 Shusaku Endo published his remarkable novel *Silence*, which quickly became a best seller in Japan and eventually a story celebrated around the world. The novel deals with the persecution of Christianity as an outlaw religion in Japan during the seventeenth century. Endo tells the story of a priest, Rodrigues, who enters Japan clandestinely and eventually comes to witness the torture of two hostages taken in the hope that local villagers might turn the priest over to the authorities. Failing in their plan, the government officials put the hostages to death by prolonged exposure to the relentless surge of the sea. Witnessing their agony from his hiding place, Rodrigues is overwhelmed by the utter silence of the sea: "What a miserable and painful business it was! The rain falls unceasingly on the sea. And the sea which killed them surges on uncannily—in silence." For Endo, however, the silence of the sea is a sign of a far deeper and a far more disturbing silence: the silence of God before the suffering of the innocent:

> What do I want to say? I myself do not quite understand. Only that today, when for the glory of God Mokichi and Ichizo [the hostages] moaned, suffered and died, I cannot bear the monotonous sound of the dark sea gnawing at the shore. Behind the depressing silence of this sea, the silence of God . . . the feeling that while men raise their voices in anguish God remains with folded arms, silent.[1]

Silence *(chinmoku)* is the governing metaphor of the entire novel. Eventually Rodrigues is captured. Faced with the unrelenting silence of God before the torture of Christian peasants suspended upside-down for days in a filthy pit, the faith of the priest takes leave of his soul. Stepping on the bronze image of Christ *(fumie)* that the authorities have placed at his feet, the priest becomes an apostate. From this point on in the novel, Endo places no more words in the priest's mouth. God's silence in the face of the priest's anguished pleading eventually leads to the priest's awful silence about God.

In the priest Rodrigues, Endo confronts us with a man on whom silence has fallen with a dreadful finality. Once full of words about God, the priest's wounded soul has lost its voice. Siddhartha Gautama, the historical Buddha, like Rodrigues, the Catholic priest, was a man silent about God. But the meaning of the Buddha's silence is of an entirely different order from that of the priest. In beginning to learn about the nature and significance of the Buddha's silence, those who read and admire Endo's insightful novel may come to look on the priest's silence in new ways.

Siddhartha Gautama was a man of momentous silences. The tradition is unanimous in holding that the Buddha refused to speak on four topics: (1) whether or not the universe is eternal, (2) whether or not the universe is finite, (3) whether or not there is a soul that exists after death, and (4) whether or not there is a soul that is identical with the body. Buddhists often refer to these issues as the indeterminate questions, because answers to them are impossible to nail down. More revealingly, the Buddhist tradition refers to these issues as the "questions that do not tend to edification." Here, the practical wisdom and the primarily religious concerns of the Buddha are easier to see. These problems are to be avoided not because intellectual debate about them goes on endlessly, but rather, because entanglement in these conundrums can actually be harmful to the one who seeks release from the world of sorrow.

It is worth pointing out that the problem of whether or not God exists is not included in the traditional list of the "questions that do not tend to edification." But to conclude from this omission that the existence of God was not an indeterminate question, or that the Buddha was an uncomplicated believer in God would be a serious mistake. Early Buddhist scriptures are not at all bashful in making mention of India's myriad gods *(devas)*. The gods, in their thousands and tens of thousands, are especially prominent in the legends surrounding the birth, renunciation, and enlightenment of the Buddha. The *devas* assist Siddhartha in escaping from his father's palace. They rejoice at the moment of the Buddha's enlightenment. Brahma, one of the three great divinities of India, pleads with the newly enlightened Buddha to turn back toward the world and begin to share his infinite wisdom with all sentient creatures still trapped in the endless cycles of karma. But on the question of the existence of God, God as generally understood by Christians, the Buddha was utterly silent.

VACCHAGOTTA'S QUESTIONS

In the oldest of the Buddhist scriptures, the Samyutta-Nikaya, there is a story regarding an encounter between the Buddha and a certain Vacchagotta, a wandering seeker. This encounter reveals much about the meaning of the Buddha's carefully chosen silences. The background to the Buddha's conversation with Vacchagotta is the debate between, on the one hand, the eternalists, who held that there was an eternal self or soul *(atman)* that was ultimately identical with the everlasting and unchanging metaphysical foundation of the universe (Brahman), and on the other hand, the nihilists or annihilationists, who denied the existence of such an eternal Self. The encounter begins with Vacchagotta approaching the Buddha with a question about the existence of an eternal Self, one of the questions, it should be noted, that "do not tend to edification":

> Then Vacchagotta, the wandering ascetic, approached the Blessed One, greeted him courteously, sat down to one side, and said: "Well, now, good Gotama, is there a Self?"
>
> The Blessed One remained silent.
>
> "Well, then, good Gotama, is there not a Self?"
>
> Once again, the Blessed One remained silent, and the wandering ascetic Vaccagotta got up and went away.

Ananda, one of the Buddha's most cherished disciples, is confused by his teacher's silence. Does silence indicate a refusal to answer on the part of the Buddha? An inability to answer? The story ends with a discussion between the Buddha and Ananda:

> Soon thereafter, the Venerable Ananda said to the Blessed One: "Master, why did you not respond to the wandering ascetic Vacchagotta's question?"
>
> "Ananda, if in response to Vacchagotta's first question I asserted that there is a Self, that would be associating myself with the renouncers and brahmins who are eternalists. But, Ananda, if in response to his second question I asserted that there is no Self, that would be associating myself with the renouncers and brahmins who are annihilationists.
>
> "Or again, Ananda, if in response to the wandering ascetic Vacchagotta's first question I asserted that there is a Self, would that be in accord with the knowledge that all elements of reality are without Self?"
>
> "No, it would not, Master."
>
> "But, Ananda, if in response to Vaccagotta's second question I asserted that there is no Self, the confused Vaccagotta would have been even more confused, saying, 'Formerly I had a Self, but now it does not exist.'"[2]

Silence is the most appropriate response to Vacchagotta's two questions not simply because the Buddha wished to avoid being associated with one side of this philosophical controversy or another. The Buddha wishes to help Vacchagotta untangle himself from the controversy itself in order to free him to seek the path that leads to release from suffering. Were the Buddha to answer yes to Vacchagotta's first question, he would have been aligning himself with the eternalists. But, contrary to the eternalists, the Buddha did not teach the existence of an eternal soul. Were the Buddha to have answered yes to Vacchagotta's second question, he would have been aligning himself with the annihilationists. But neither did the Buddha teach the nonexistence of an eternal soul.

In presenting this text, Buddhist teachers often ask what if the Buddha answered yes to Vacchagotta's second question, "Is there not a Self?" Indeed, the Buddha never taught the existence of an eternal soul. But answering yes might lead Vacchagotta to conclude that the Buddha wanted to assert the existence of some kind of non-soul *(anatman)* in contrast to a soul *(atman)*. This would be to place the Buddha within the camp of the annihilationists in opposition to the eternalists. Neither a yes answer nor a no answer would have been helpful to Vacchagotta or true to the Buddha's teaching. Thus the wisest response, and as

Buddhists say, the most compassionate response, was the Buddha's actual response: silence.

And silence is a real response to Vacchagotta. The Buddha's intention is not to duck the question by taking no position at all. His silence is carefully, skillfully calculated to serve Vacchagotta's real needs. The Buddha's silence opens up for Vacchagotta the possibility of a middle path between what the Buddha saw as two extreme positions. In the story the Buddha neither affirms nor denies the existence of an eternal soul. Neither does the Buddha affirm nor deny the nonexistence of a soul. Moreover, the Buddha says nothing about some third position that would serve as an alternative to the first two positions. Instead, the Buddha's answer to Vacchagotta is a calculated silence about a metaphysical conundrum, an indeterminate question that, moreover, does not tend to edification. Speculation for its own sake about metaphysical problems can easily become a substitute for the religious quest for enlightenment.

What if Vacchagotta had asked about the existence of God instead of the existence of the soul? As mentioned above, early Buddhist scriptures are full of references to the gods *(devas)*. These supernatural beings should not be equated with what Christians mean when they use the word *God*. Although they lead happier and less encumbered lives than lesser creatures, the *devas* are as much entangled in *samsara*, the world of suffering, as any human being. Like all sentient beings, the *devas* are born and eventually die and are subject to the karmic law of rebirth. The Christian God, therefore, cannot be considered a *deva*, or even the highest of the *devas*. Christianity's God is not a sentient being but rather the Creator of sentient beings, the Supreme Being. It is precisely this Christian understanding of God that the Buddha passes over in silence.

In India, debates about the nature of universe and the soul have tended to eclipse the problem of God. Or perhaps more accurately, in the West people ask if God really exists, whereas in India people ask about the relationship between the soul and the universe. In the days of the Buddha the eternalists argued that the highest truth of the soul *(atman)* was its unity with all of reality itself (Brahman). The annihilationists rejected this teaching with views that were materialistic and, some were arguing, nihilistic. Metaphysical views about the existence of Ultimate Reality such as these provoked the Buddha's skillful use of silence. The Buddha was not silent about *devas*. The *devas* were as much a part of his world as human beings and animals. But the *devas* are not equivalent to the Ultimate Reality of Brahman in Hindu thought or to the Supreme Being of Christianity. With all the Buddha's easy talk about the gods, Christians should not overlook the Buddha's utter silence about God.

Is there a Supreme Being who has created all, who judges all, who saves all? Is there an eternal soul that is one with an eternal universe? Does the world and everything in the world, including ourselves, have a metaphysical foundation? Asked to respond to such questions, the Buddha offered neither a yes nor a no. Only silence. Karl Marx was not silent in regard to the question of the existence of God. God does not exist, he tells us, especially in his early writings. Belief in God was itself a symptom of a society suffering from the disease of economic and political injustice. Even so, Marx was more of an anti-theist than an atheist.

He wanted to turn our faith away from a distracting but useless God in heaven so that we might place our faith in the ultimate truth of society's inevitable material development. Quite as much as any God-fearing Christian, Marx believed in the existence of an Ultimate Reality. For Marx, the Ultimate Reality was the dialectical development of matter. Neither was Friedrich Nietzsche silent about God. In proclaiming the "death of God," Nietzsche's Madman shouts to all the world that we have "reached out and erased the horizon!" But we tend to forget that the death of God in the modern world was not good news for Nietzsche. God's death leaves modern human beings with a terrible burden; since all is meaninglessness and abyss, every individual must dominate the abyss by creating his or her own meaning. In stark contrast to the Buddha's sense of the extinction of ego-centered living, Nietzsche makes the ego absolute. No wonder he had such harsh words for Buddhism.[3]

A MULTITUDE OF OPINIONS

Both within Buddhism and outside of it, the stories recounting the Buddha's silence have generated a great deal of controversy. How should we interpret the meaning of this silence? If words so often lend themselves to a multiplicity of interpretations, how much more will silence generate a conflict of interpretations?

Some commentators have interpreted the Buddha's silence as a form of philosophical agnosticism about Ultimate Reality, including the existence or nonexistence of God.[4] In this view the Buddha's enlightenment did not include any insight into the metaphysical foundation of things. Thus for the Buddha and for anyone who should attain enlightenment, the indeterminate questions remain indeterminate: no final position regarding the existence of a soul and its foundation in Brahman is possible. This view of the Buddha's silence is bolstered somewhat by the fact that the tradition has assigned the question of the existence of an eternal soul to the dustbin of indeterminate questions.

However, agnosticism as an interpretation of the Buddha's silence is unsatisfactory for several reasons. For one, if the Buddha did not in fact know the answer to Vacchagotta's question, what would it have cost him simply to say so? If the historical Buddha was in fact an agnostic regarding metaphysical and theological problems, what was the purpose served by this curious silence? Furthermore, the Buddha never claimed he was an agnostic. In fact, at times the Buddhist tradition suggests his enlightenment blessed him with omniscience. There is the following scriptural passage, also in the Samyutta-Nikaya, which asserts that the Buddha knew much more than he actually taught his disciples:

Once the Exalted One was staying at Kosambi in Simsapa Grove. Then the Exalted One, gathering up a few simsapa leaves in his hands, said to the monks:

"What think ye, monks? Which are the more numerous, just this mere handful of simsapa leaves I have here, or those in the grove overhead?"

"Very few in number, lord, are the leaves in the handful gathered up by the Exalted One; much more in number are those in the grove overhead."

"Just so, monks, much more in number are those things I have found out but not revealed."

There is much about which the Buddha has decided to say nothing. Maybe the Buddha's silence before Vacchagotta was motivated by a religious purpose rather than an inability to find an answer to the question. The Buddha may have had Vacchagotta's best interests in mind when he chose silence as a response. What religious purpose would be served by such silence? The text provides an answer:

And why, monks, have I not revealed them? Because they are not con-cerned with profit, they are not rudiments of the holy life, they conduce not to revulsion, to dispassion, to cessation, to tranquillity, to full comprehen-sion, to the perfect wisdom, to Nibbana [nirvana]. That is why I have not revealed them.[5]

The silence of the Buddha is not dictated by any lack of knowledge. There is much he knows that he does not tell. Nor can his silence be seen as a power game played by a religious charlatan. He remains silent about that which is not useful to Vacchagotta for following the path that leads to enlightenment. Given the pro-pensity of human beings to become embroiled in metaphysical disputes that dis-tract from the religious quest for wisdom, the most sensible course, indeed the most compassionate course, is to remain silent.

Can the meaning of the Buddha's silence be found in some form of mystical experience?[6] This position has myriad supporters, including not a few Christians involved in interreligious dialogue with Buddhists. William Johnston has written extensively on the parallels between Buddhist thought and the mysticism of John of the Cross and Teresa of Avila.[7] Hans Waldenfels, in a book that compares the Christian theology of Karl Rahner with the contemporary Buddhist thought of Keiji Nishitani, argues that the mystical experience of Ultimate Reality as an incomprehensible Mystery is the common ground on which Buddhists and Chris-tians can meet for interreligious dialogue.[8] Ultimate Reality, the metaphysical foundation out of which all things arise, is incomprehensible and cannot be grasped by means of any finite concept. Thus when Rahner, the Christian theologian, speaks of "holy Mystery" and when Nishitani, the Buddhist philosopher, speaks of "Absolute Nothingness," in fact, Waldenfels claims, they are using differing expressions for the same mystical experience of Ultimate Reality.

Mysticism, however, is a notoriously slippery term. In his later years, D. T. Suzuki, the first great exponent of Zen Buddhism in the West, regretted his ear-lier writings in which he explained Zen as a form of mysticism.[9] If mysticism entails some form of intuitive knowledge of the Ultimate Reality or divine Mys-tery that lies beyond this world as its foundation, then the Buddha's silence should not be called mystical. Some forms of Hinduism, especially the spiritual systems derived from the Upanishads and their teachings about Brahman, are more easily compared with Christian mysticism. In both cases there is some form of unity of the soul with Ultimate Reality. The silence of the mystic results from the complete inadequacy of any word or concept to capture the overwhelming experience of the ineffable, whether Brahman or God. But the Buddha's silence about God or Brahman is not the mystic's silence. His silence does not point to the existence of a transcendent ultimate that lies beyond words. He was as silent about the existence of God as he was about God's nonexistence. When the Buddha refuses to respond to Vacchagotta's metaphysical questions, and even more to the point, when the question of the existence of God is not even raised in the early Buddhist scriptures, it is not because the Buddha has had an intuition into the ultimately real that cannot be put into words. In fact, the Buddha's silence does not derive from a mystical intuition into a transcendent Ultimate Reality at all. Rather it derives from the Buddha's compassion toward Vacchagotta; neither a yes nor a no answer to Vacchagotta will do him any good. Thus the silence of the Buddha cannot be simply equated with the silence of the mystic (Christian or otherwise) before the Ineffable and the Ultimate.

Was the Buddha simply uninterested in metaphysical problems of any sort? This would seem to make him into a suspiciously modern and Western type of thinker. Some modern philosophers like A. J. Ayer and John Wisdom hold that metaphysical statements about Ultimate Reality as well as theological statements about God are not so much wrong as just plain meaningless. Since metaphysical and theological statements can neither be verified nor falsified by observation, the truth or falsity of statements like "God exists" cannot be decided one way or another. When metaphysical or theological questions arise, the most sensible course of action is simply to change the subject. Such an interpretation of the Buddha's silence is not as implausible as it may sound at first. Some of the Buddha's modern interpreters have identified him as a very strict empiricist. In calling the issues raised by Vacchagotta the indeterminate questions, the Buddhist tradition seems to be in agreement with those modern philosophers who reject as meaningless statements that cannot be empirically verified.[10]

But in addition to calling Vacchagotta's issues the indeterminate questions, the tradition also refers to them as the questions that do not tend to edification. This latter designation leads us back to the Buddha's essentially religious concerns and a religious interpretation of the silence. The silence does not indicate a philosophical rejection of metaphysics and theology as illogical or meaningless but rather a refocusing of our attention back on to the religious path that leads to enlightenment.

A STRATEGIC SILENCE

The Buddha's silent response to Vacchagotta indicates neither agnosticism nor mysticism nor a logical rejection of metaphysics and theology as meaningless. In responding to Vacchagotta the Buddha refrains from speaking in order to achieve a religious end: helping his disciples in attaining freedom from suffering. This point is well illustrated by the "poison arrow sermon" of the Buddha.

In the Majhima-Nikaya, another collection of the early Sutras, a disciple named Malunkyaputta asks the Buddha for a definitive answer to the questions that do not tend to edification raised by Vacchagotta. In contrast to the Vacchagotta story, this time the Buddha does not respond with silence but rather scolds Malunkyaputta for having become entangled in the trap of metaphysical speculation for its own sake. The Buddha likens his disciple's state to the foolishness of a man who was wounded by a poison-tipped arrow during a battle. When his companions began to remove the arrow, the man began to object in surprising ways:

> I will not have the arrow drawn out until I know the one who pierced me, whether he is a nobleman or a Brahman, a merchant or a laborer. . . . What is his name, and to which clan does he belong? I will not have the arrow drawn out until I know the type of bow with which I was pierced, whether it is a spring-bow or a cross-bow. . . .

With an arrow in his gut and poison surging through his veins toward his heart, the mortally wounded man is asking all the wrong questions. The man is not only impractical, he is behaving in a way that is physically dangerous to himself. So too, Malunkyaputta's metaphysical interests are not only impractical but dangerous as well, for they distract him from what is of paramount importance: following the path that leads to enlightenment. The Buddha explains the image to his disciple:

> In the same way, Malunkyaputta, whoever should speak thus: "I will not [follow the path of the Lord Buddha] until the Lord explains to me either that the world is eternal or that the world is not eternal . . . " this man might pass away, Malunkyaputta, or ever it was explained to him.

Speculation on metaphysical questions becomes an obstacle to enlightenment when it becomes a substitute for the religious quest to find release from suffering. The path that leads to the ending of suffering cannot be reduced to any metaphysical view about ultimate reality. Questions such as Malunkyaputta's lead to endless debate and not to the release from the labyrinth of sorrow that is *samsara*:

> [Following in the path of the Buddha,] Malunkyaputta, could not be said to depend on the view that the world is eternal. Nor could [following in the path of the Buddha] be said to depend on the view that the world is not eternal. Whether there is the view that the world is eternal or whether there is the view that the world is not eternal, there is birth, there is aging, there is dying, there are grief, sorrow, suffering, lamentation, and despair, the suppression of which I lay down here and now.[11]

The Buddha's silence regarding the indeterminate questions, indeed, his silence about God, should not be mistaken for an intellectual agnosticism. Neither should it be seen as mystical silence based on an intuition of a transcendent Ultimate Reality. And since the Buddha's silence is in the service of a religious quest for enlightenment, neither can it be interpreted simply as a rejection of metaphysics and theology as meaningless. The religious quest for release from suffering cannot be replaced by the intellectual quest for a correct theory about the nature of reality. But neither can it be replaced by a nihilistic rejection of metaphysical theories. In responding to Vacchagotta with silence, the Buddha has a religious purpose in mind. He wants to protect his disciples from the temptation of substituting conceptual abstractions for the real experience of religious awakening. We might call this silence practical, or even strategic. It is a silence that neither rejects metaphysics nor embraces it, neither denies the existence of a soul or Ultimate Reality or God nor affirms them. Rather, it is a silence that takes a middle path that embraces neither yes nor no in order to clear away the distractions that keep us from what is the real quest: the liberation from suffering.

THE LIFE OF SIDDHARTHA GAUTAMA

Siddhartha Gautama, the historical Buddha, must be counted among the most influential human beings ever to have lived on the Indian subcontinent. This statement remains true even now, some twenty-five centuries after his birth in the foothills of the Himalayas. Some of the most important traditions regarding the life of Siddhartha Gautama were eventually assembled into a text known as the "Introduction to the Jatakas." Although these stories are sometimes contradictory and unreliable as information regarding the historical Buddha, the values and insights enshrined in these stories speak eloquently about the followers of the Buddha who tell these stories to honor him.[12]

Even before his birth into the aristocracy of the Sakya clan in either 624 or 448 BC,[13] Siddhartha was the cause of controversy. Soothsayers had predicted that the child would grow up to be either a universal ruler *(Chakravartin)* or a universal religious teacher *(Buddha)*. The king was eventually told that he must shield his son from suffering in order to ensure that the child grow to be a universal ruler. The experience of suffering would lead the prince to set off on the religious quest that would eventually lead to Buddhahood. Great walls of pleasure were built around the child, and no expense was spared in the king's attempt to inoculate his son from the experience of suffering. But in the Buddhist view of things, intoxication with worldly pleasures does not bring peace of mind. The more the king was successful at shielding his son from the reality of suffering, the more the prince became inwardly unhappy.

Siddhartha's restlessness led him to make a series of four excursions over the palace wall with his friend and charioteer, Channa. On the first journey beyond the pleasure palace, Siddhartha encountered an old man, bent and feeble with age, on the way to a village festival. Siddhartha asks Channa a question arising out of his naive lack of acquaintance with suffering:

Good charioteer, who is this man with white hair, supporting himself on the staff in his hand, with his eyes veiled by the brows, and limbs relaxed and bent? Is this some transformation in him, or his original state, or mere chance?

Channa's answer spares no expense in driving home its terrifying point:

Old age it is called, that which has broken him down—the murderer of beauty, the ruin of vigor, the birthplace of sorrow, the grave of pleasure, the destroyer of memory, the enemy of the senses.

Siddhartha's naiveté is shaken by the whole experience:

[The prince] sighed deeply and shook his head, and looking on the festive multitude he uttered these word in his perturbation: "Thus old age strikes down indiscriminately memory and beauty and valor, and yet with such a sight before its eyes the world is not perturbed. This being so, turn back the horses, charioteer; go quickly home again. For how can I take my pleasure in the garden, when the fear of old age rules my mind?"[14]

This first encounter with an old man is followed by subsequent encounters with a sick man and a dead man. On his fourth trip over the wall, Siddhartha meets up with a holy man, a wandering ascetic, in the forest, composed and at peace. The first three encounters left the prince unhinged. This fourth encounter sets in motion a great resolve in the prince to seek release from anxiety for himself.

In what is now known as the Buddha's "Great Renunciation" *(Mahabhiniskramana)*, Siddhartha trades the prison of pleasure his father's palace had become for a life of homeless wandering in search of release from the bondage of suffering. In the Gospels, Jesus teaches his disciples that "the birds have their nest, the foxes have their lair, but the Son of Man has no place to lay his head" (Mt 8:20). This sense of homelessness expounded by Jesus is intensified when we read of his rejection by his fellow villagers in Nazareth (Mk 6:1–6) and becomes downright troubling when we hear the story of his mother and brothers trying to convince him to give up his public ministry and return home. Jesus' response is to ask, "Who is my mother? Who are my brothers?" (Mt 12:46–50). Homelessness, as the life of the Buddha indicates, is an important religious value for Buddhists as well. Reflecting on this turning point in his life, the Buddha speaks to his monks:

Then I, monks, after a time, being young, my hair coal-black, possessed of radiant youth, in the prime of my life—although my unwilling parents wept and wailed—having cut off my hair and beard, having put on yellow robes, went forth from home into homelessness.[15]

The movement into homelessness, the result of a voluntary renunciation, is one of the major themes to be found among the traditions surrounding the life of

Siddhartha Gautama. This is due in no small part to the fact that these stories serve as models for the monastic lives of nuns and monks.[16] In entering the monastic life, a novice must leave the familiar world of family and friends. Ordinary clothes are abandoned for the saffron robe. In Thailand, even a novice from a poor family is given fine robes to wear to his initiation ceremony, only that they might be discarded for the simple saffron robes of the *samgha* (monastic order). The head is shaved, indicating the renunciation of caste standing. Mother and father, marriage and household are renounced for the "homelessness" of the monastery. That monastic life, seen as a kind of spiritual homelessness, has deep roots in Buddhist tradition. In the Majhima-Nikaya the Buddha describes the renunciation he expects of his disciples:

> After a time, getting rid of his mass of wealth, whether large or small, getting rid of his circle of relations, whether large or small, having had his hair and beard shaved, having donned saffron robes, he goes forth from home into homelessness.[17]

Homelessness is not destitution. It is not involuntary. In fact, homelessness is the basis on which the monk begins the spiritual quest for enlightenment. It is non-attachment to the distractions of the world. Like Jesus speaking of the Son of man, the Buddha invites his disciples to a special kind of homelessness.

Setting off into the world beyond the walls of his father's palace, the young prince, now the young renouncer, began to trade a life of extreme pleasure for a life of extreme asceticism. He became the leader of a group of five renouncers noteworthy for their ferocious austerities. At one point the emaciated former prince could take hold of his backbone through his stomach, a point dramatically depicted in Buddhist statuary. The Buddha spoke of this time of his life as follows:

> All my limbs became like the knotted joints of withered creepers, my buttocks like a bullock's hoof, my protruding backbone like a string of balls, my gaunt ribs like the crazy rafters of a tumble-down shed. My eyes lay deep in their sockets, their pupils sparkling like water in a deep well. As an unripe gourd shrivels and shrinks in a hot wind, so became my scalp. If I thought, "I will touch the skin of my belly," it was the skin of my backbone that I also took hold of, since the skin of my belly and back met. The hairs, rotting at the roots, fell away from my body when I stroked my limbs.[18]

After collapsing into unconsciousness and then awakening, Siddhartha realized that extreme asceticism was as useless in finding release from the problem of suffering and death as the extremes of hedonism that had made up his earlier life. The future Buddha resolved to find a middle path between these two extremes. With this aim in mind, Siddhartha began to take nourishment again by accepting some milk offered by a woman named Nandabala (or in some traditions Sujata), the daughter of a cow-herder. With this, his disciples deserted him for his betrayal of their strict asceticism. Now all alone, Siddhartha sat down beneath a banyan tree and began a meditation that, after forty-nine days, would end in enlightenment. During this time Siddhartha was sorely tempted by Mara, the demon of worldly pleasures, and his three daughters. Reminiscent of Jesus' temptation in the desert, Mara tries to distract Siddhartha from his mission with the promise of universal empire. On the forty-ninth day, through the three watches of the night, Siddhartha became an enlightened being, or Buddha.

On the first watch the Buddha began to recall his previous births: first his life before his birth as Siddhartha, then the life before that, then hundreds and thousands of previous lives. In the second watch the Buddha gained insight into the suffering of all sentient beings through the countless cycles of their own death and rebirth. According to Buddhist teaching, a sentient being may be reborn on any of six different levels of life from the deepest hell to the highest of heavens. But even those who are reborn in heaven are subject to rebirth. Heaven itself, no matter how delightful, is still a part of the vast realm of *samsara*. In the third watch the Buddha gained insight into the four Noble Truths that form the core of the Buddha's forty-five years of preaching in the lower Ganges River basin.

After his enlightenment the Buddha was completely free, no longer attached to things of this world in any way that would produce suffering. As a fully enlightened one (Buddha), Siddhartha was no longer compelled to forge fetters of karma binding him to *samsara* and no longer bound to the world in any way. According to one tradition, the gods appeared to the Buddha in order to beg him to return to the world and to preach the *dharma* (the "law" or "truth" of Buddhism). At first the Buddha refused, arguing that no one could understand a tiny fraction of the truth of his enlightenment. The gods persist and the Buddha finally relents. The Buddha thus began a new kind of relationship with the world, no longer based on obsessions and attachments, but rather a relationship with the world based on infinite compassion. Out of this "great compassion" *(mahakaruna)* the Buddha began to preach. Starting at the Deer Park in Varanasi (near modern day Banaras, in northeast India), the Buddha rejoined the five ascetics who had abandoned him in disgust.

There is widespread agreement among Buddhists that the Buddha preached for forty-five years. During this time he gathered hundreds if not thousands of disciples. The various materials concerned with the preaching of the Buddha offer a wealth of miracle stories, sermons, and anecdotes regarding his encounters with many kinds of people. Like the gospel texts in Christianity, these accounts may or may not be based on actual historical events. Whether or not these texts have a historical basis, they certainly reflect the beliefs of the Buddhist community after the time of the historical Buddha. In this respect as well, early Buddhist scriptures are similar to the Gospels.

When being precise, Buddhists do not speak of their teacher's "death" at the end of his teaching career. Instead of dying the Buddha is said to have passed into his "final nirvana" *(parinirvana)*. Buddhists sometimes distinguish between enlightenment with a body and enlightenment without a body. After his awakening the Buddha was enlightened with a body. This allowed him to teach within the world. *Parinirvana* is the continuation of the Buddha's enlightenment without a body. Like all composite things, the Buddha's body was a construct that eventually came to be deconstructed by the natural flow of events. After the *parinirvana*, enlightenment continues without the body. The notion of a *parinirvana*, as opposed to a death, is a Buddhist way of observing that the Buddha, as an enlightened one, was no longer subject to the cycle of death and rebirth. In time the Buddhist community settled on the title Tathagata for the Buddha, a term which may mean "thus come, thus gone." This title signifies that the Buddha is neither alive nor dead, neither present in the world as an object nor in another world beyond this one like a god.

NOBLE TRUTHS

After his enlightenment the Buddha is said to have made a decision of crucial importance. Perfectly liberated, the Buddha could have chosen to remain contentedly within his bliss, utterly set free from all attachments to the world. Instead, in an act that Buddhists see as the perfection of enlightened wisdom by compassion, the Buddha decided to share his truth with the world. According to the tradition the Buddha's first sermon, also known as "the setting in motion of the wheel of the *Dharma*," was delivered to his five monks at Sarnath near contemporary Banaras.[19] The first words of the Buddha set forth four Noble Truths. First, life is fundamentally unsatisfactory and riddled with suffering *(dukkha)*. Second, *dukkha* has an origin. It arises simultaneously with our passions, thirsts, desires, and obsessions. Third, since *dukkha* has an origin, it also has an end. *Dukkha* ends when desire ends. Fourth, the way that leads to the extinguishing of *dukkha* is the eightfold path, the practices that form the center of the life of the *samgha*, the monastic community founded by the Buddha.

FIRST NOBLE TRUTH: *DUKKHA*

The first of the Noble Truths teaches that all of life is *dukkha*, that is, unsatisfactory and afflicted with suffering. In addition to "unsatisfactory" and "suffering," *dukkha* might also be translated as "sorrow" or "unease." Life itself is *dukkha*. The claim is more radical than it may seem at first. All is *dukkha*, not merely old age, sickness, and death, nor simply our involvement with what is unpleasant, or not getting what we want. Consciousness itself is *dukkha*:

> Now, monks, what is the Noble Truth of suffering [*dukkha*]? Just this: Birth is suffering, old age is suffering, sickness is suffering, death is suffering. Involvement with what is unpleasant is suffering. Also, not getting what one wants and strives for is suffering. And form is suffering, feeling is suffering, perception is suffering, karmic constituents are suffering, consciousness is suffering; in sum, these five agglomerations, which are the basis of clinging to existence, are suffering. This, monks, is the Noble Truth of suffering.[20]

There is happiness, to be sure, such as health and beauty, prosperity and the pleasures of the senses. But happiness, all happiness, is fleeting, not lasting. Thus, in the end, even happiness is unsatisfactory.

To take this basic Buddhist teaching as a fatalistic view of our human situation, however, would be a mistake. Rather than pessimism, the Noble Truth of suffering is a kind of doctor's diagnosis that comes before the prescription to treat the disease. *Dukkha* results when we cling to things as if they were everlasting. The mind has a deeply rooted propensity to become attached to things. Since these things will eventually come to an end, human existence is unsatisfactory. For this reason the notion of *dukkha* is intimately connected with the early Buddhist theory of the origin and interrelatedness of all things: dependent arising *(pratitya-samutpada)*.

The doctrine of dependent arising has two aspects, each with important ramifications. The first has to do with the radical interdependence of all. The second has to do the radical transience of all.

In Buddhist teaching, all things cause all other things to come into being and to pass out of being. From this it follows that all of reality is a single network of infinitely complex interrelationships in which each and every thing is interdependent. Everything depends on everything else for its existence. It follows then that nothing is absolute. Nothing exists of its own. All is relative. The world is a whirlwind of interconnected parts, each the cause of all the others. When one part arises, other parts arise. When that one part ceases, the other parts cease. Every part of reality is dependent on each and every other part of reality.

This Buddhist theory of causality can be contrasted with the ancient Greek understanding of the reality of things, which has had such an impact on the Christian worldview and especially the Christian understanding of God. Buddhists think of reality as if it were a tripod of sticks. Each separate stick, by holding up the other two, can be said to cause the tripod to be. Remove any of the three sticks, and there no longer is a tripod.[21] Reality, of course, is considerably more complex. If the universe is a tripod, it is a tripod with an unimaginable number of legs. All this relativity and mutuality has no one single foundation. Just as no one particular leg of the tripod holds up the whole tripod by itself, so also, there is no one part of reality that is more fundamental than any other part. Thus in the early Sutras, there is no mention of Being Itself, or a Prime Mover, as in Greek philosophy. In the Greek understanding of causality, there are some aspects of reality that are more fundamental, more basic, more necessary than other parts of reality. Being Itself, for example, is the cause of the existence of all the individual beings that exist. Aristotle spoke of a Prime Mover who is the cause of all movement in the world but is not moved by anything. Christian theologians used these Greek ideas to explain their belief in a Creator. God is not merely a being among other beings in the world. God is the Supreme Being, the cause and foundation of all things that exist. God is the Prime Mover, the unmoved mover of all. Buddhism, unlike Christianity, has no notion of the "Maker of heaven and of earth," the Creator-God who has brought the world into being and who one day will bring creation to an end. Instead, Buddhism imagines reality to be the cause of itself, with no God beyond it as its transcendent Creator.

The second aspect of the doctrine of dependent arising emphasizes the fact that all of reality is radically transient *(anicca)*. Everything is always in a state of becoming. Things are constantly arising and ceasing, causing and being caused. Nothing is eternal. Nothing endures. All is in the process of coming into being, lasting for a time and then falling into oblivion. The world is nothing more than one utterly momentary state of affairs passing into another. Not only are beauty and pleasure passing, but grief and sorrow are as well. Any belief to the contrary is illusion.

Now we can see how intimately connected the doctrine of dependent arising is with the first Noble Truth, *dukkha*. The world as envisioned in the doctrine of dependent arising is a perilous place for anyone who clings to some finite part of the world as if it were eternal. Living this way courts inevitable suffering and is fundamentally unsatisfactory. And yet we continue to cling to finite things within the world obstinately and passionately, even when we see that our attachments do not bring us happiness. Similarly, the doctrine does not encourage us to transcend the world by fastening on to some unchanging Absolute that lies beyond the world. There is no transcendent and eternal Absolute beyond the world in which we might find respite. Buddhism is silent about the existence of a Creator-God as in Christian belief. Instead, everything arises dependently. Everything is the cause of everything else.

Should *dukkha* be thought of as a form of evil? This would be a mistake. *Dukkha* is not evil in any moral sense. *Dukkha* is not a sin. Likewise, it would be a mistake to think of *dukkha* as evil in any metaphysical sense. In this, Christianity and Buddhism are of one mind: the world is not evil. Instead of evil, Buddhists simply teach that all things are unsatisfactory. *Dukkha* is not a sin that results from breaking the rules, not a Manichean "dark side" of reality that menaces us even as we try to escape into the light. Instead, *dukkha* has to do with our inability to live contentedly with ourselves in a world that will not stand still for us and do what we want it to do. It is our lack of equanimity. It has more to do with our psychology than our moral failures or the metaphysical character of reality. "Our hearts are restless," wrote Augustine in his *Confessions*, "until they rest in Thee." Buddhists certainly agree with the first part of Augustine's claim. We are not at war with reality. We are at war with ourselves. *Dukkha* is the inevitable outcome of this war.

SECOND NOBLE TRUTH: *SAMUDAYA*

Is Buddhism too pessimistic in its view of suffering? Hinduism, perhaps it can be said, seeks to transcend suffering. Christianity, many would agree, seeks to embrace it on the cross and see it vanquished by the grace of God. Buddhism, in contrast, seeks "to root it out at its origin." Despite their many differences, all three of these great religious traditions are in agreement that suffering is not inherent in reality itself. The origin of suffering has to do with our relationship with reality. Ultimately, we are the cause of our own suffering. Buddhism, however, cannot be said to be pessimistic. The first Noble Truth teaches that suffering is all-pervasive. The second Noble Truth comes as both a challenge and good news: since suffering has an origin, it also has an ending.

Dukkha has an origin *(samudaya)*. The Buddha located this origin in a craving, a desire, in which we become attached to the transitory things of this world:

> And what is the [second] Noble Truth of the origination of suffering? It is thirst for further existence, which comes along with pleasure and passion and brings passing enjoyment here and there. This, monks, is the Noble Truth of the origination of suffering.[22]

What is this "thirst for further existence"? In the second Noble Truth the Buddha gives a diagnosis of the human predicament that goes to the heart of the matter. We cannot abide what is. We crave for what is not. Above all, we must escape death by asserting ourselves as an enduring self by attaching ourselves to what we take to be eternal. Existence itself, then, takes the form of craving, desire, attachment, and "thirst for further existence." All our obsessions with money, power, prestige, and sex are but concrete instances of the most basic craving, the "thirst for further existence." According to the doctrine of dependent arising, nothing is eternal. All is radically transient, relative, and temporary. From this it follows that the person who would have reality stand still for his or her own purposes is asking for trouble. A life that clings to the temporal as if it were eternal soon becomes dominated with longing, disappointment, resentment, fear, and unfilled craving. Life lived obsessively is *dukkha.*

At the heart of this "thirst for further existence" is a false view of the self as an eternally enduring soul. Behind our thinking we presume there is a thinker. Behind our feelings we presume there is a feeler. Within the body we presume there is an abiding entity, an unchanging reality, what Christians generally call a soul. Even if the Buddha considered belief in a soul to be a "false view," he did not preach the nonexistence of a soul *(anatman)* as an alternative to belief in the existence of such a soul *(atman)*. Once again, the Buddha's silent response to Vacchagotta's questions is telling. Vacchagotta asks if the Buddha teaches that there is a self. The Buddha's response was silence. Does the Buddha teach that there in fact is no such thing as a soul? Once again, silence. The Buddha's silence, which disavows both eternalism (the existence of a soul) and annihilationism (the nihilistic alternative), focuses out attention on the problem of the false views we have of our situation in the world.

If the Buddha did not affirm the existence of an eternal soul, what can be the source of our experience of being an individual self? How do false views arise? Instead of an abiding and unified soul, the Buddha saw a whirlwind of separate elements constantly coming together to create the illusion of being an individual self. Our false views, therefore, arise like everything else—by means of the mechanism of dependent arising. In the generations that followed the Buddha, the

Buddhist community devised elaborate theories for explaining precisely how this false view of the self arises. The experience of being a self was broken down into five "aggregates" *(skandhas)* which cause one another by arising dependently. The countless permutations of these five aggregates account for all the various qualities of human experience. The five aggregates can be translated roughly as form or body *(rupa)*, feeling *(vedana)*, perceptions *(samjna)*, conditioning *(samskara)*, and consciousness *(vijnana)*. These five aggregates are the basis of the illusion we have of being a separate, individual self and the false views we have of the world and ourselves. Moment by moment the five aggregates arise in one configuration or another giving the illusion of a subject (an "I") that endures through time. The "I," however, cannot be identified with any of the aggregates. The "I" is an illusion created by the dependent arising of the aggregates.

Early Buddhist literature offers a famous story that illustrates the Buddhist understanding of the illusion of the self, "King Malinda's Chariot." The story is a dialogue between King Malinda and the monk Nagasena. Their conversation has to do with a technical debate within the Buddhist community about the existence of a subtle "person" *(puggala)* that exists apart from the body. The story, however, ably illustrates Buddhist teaching about the arising of the illusion of the self as an ever-changing configuration of aggregates.[23] Arguing against the existence of a higher, transcendent self or "person," Nagasena asks the king to think of the illusion of being a self as something that can be broken down into parts, like the king's own chariot. "Is the axle the chariot? . . . the wheels? . . . the yoke?" the king is asked. No, it is not. "Then, your majesty, is it something other than the axle . . . the wheels . . . the yoke?" The answer is again no. Eventually the king comes to an insight. "The word *chariot* comes into existence," the king realizes, "dependent on the axle . . . the wheels . . . the yoke; it is a designation, a description, an appellation, a name." And it is nothing more; the chariot has no independent existence apart from aggregates that make it up. Moreover, the chariot cannot be reduced to any one of its constituent parts. The axle is not the whole chariot; neither is the wheel. Most important for this analogy, when any single part is removed, the chariot ceases to exist. Like the tripod of sticks mentioned above in connection with the principle of dependent arising, all the parts working together make the chariot to be a chariot. Like tripods and chariots, the false view of ourselves as an eternal soul arises as a constellation of aggregates. But even the false view of the self as a thing that exists all by itself is a part of the flux and flow of *samsara*. It too is a fabrication.

Life lived in terms of false views has brought about much that is violent and abhorrent in the course of time. The false views we have of the self correspond to the false views we have of money, power, prestige, gender, race, ethnicity, and all the other obsessions that are driven by "thirst for further existence." The origin of *dukkha* is desire, according to the second Noble Truth. Desire is not a brute and incomprehensible fact. Desire is a sign of false views of reality, which in turn can be factored into component parts. As these components have an origin, so also they have an ending. The ending of desire brings us to the third Noble Truth.

THE THIRD NOBLE TRUTH: *NIRODHA*

The third of the four Noble Truths has to do with the ending or ceasing *(nirodha)* of *dukkha*. Since *dukkha* has an origin, it also has an ending. The ending of *dukkha* lies in the quelling of craving and the severing of attachment. Therefore, there is the real possibility of finding liberation from suffering:

> And what is the [third] Noble Truth of the cessation of suffering? It is this: the destruction without remainder of this very thirst for further existence, which comes along with pleasure and passion, bringing passing enjoyment here and there. It is without passion. It is cessation, forsaking, abandoning, renunciation. This, monks, is the Noble Truth of the cessation of suffering.[24]

Suffering arises with thirst. Suffering ceases when thirst ceases. *Dukkha* is a sign of attachment. *Dukkha* ceases when attachment is severed. Therefore, practices having to do with the forsaking, abandoning or renunciation of craving also have to do with bringing to an end the unsatisfactory state of affairs that is recognized in the first Noble Truth.

In order to eliminate *dukkha* completely, one must uproot it at its point of origin, the thirst for further existence. The complete extinction of this most basic of all thirsts brings with it the complete extinction of suffering. Buddhists call this nirvana. How might one describe this event? Buddhists are often quick to insist that nirvana is beyond words. Walhola Rahula, author of a classic introduction to Buddhist thought, notes that since a fish has no word for land, the tortoise cannot explain to the fish why one does not swim on dry land.[25] Not surprisingly, instead of trying to name nirvana directly with words, Buddhists have generally preferred to speak about what nirvana is not. Thus it is often spoken of as not constructed *(akrta)* and thus a state very much unlike the illusion of the everlasting self, which is constructed. In fact, to deconstruct the illusion of being a separate, individual self is to deconstruct the mechanism through which thirst for further existence generates *dukkha*. To deconstruct the illusion of the self, therefore, is to deconstruct the mechanism that generates suffering. This state of being deconstructed or not constructed is called nirvana.

Buddhists also talk about nirvana as the extinction of *dukkha*. The term *nirvana* is related to the Sanskrit verb *nirva*, which means "to be extinguished" or "to be burned out." From this comes the notion of nirvana as the "extinction" or "annihilation" of craving or the "destruction without remainder of this very thirst for further existence" in accord with the third Noble Truth. Thus early Buddhist scriptures speak of the extinction of desire *(ragakkhayo)*, the extinction of hatred *(dosakkhayo)*, and the extinction of illusions *(mohakkhayo)*.[26]

But herein also lies a danger of misunderstanding. Nirvana should not be understood as an effect resulting from a cause or as a result gained at the end of a long period of effort. Nirvana is not a goal that is achieved. We can say that an athlete, after much effort, succeeds in running a four-minute mile. A medical student, with much study and preparation, succeeds in becoming a doctor. A Buddhist, however, does not succeed in realizing nirvana. Ultimately, there is running but no runner. There is study but no separate self that studies. There is enlightenment but no soul or self that is enlightened. As a verb, *nirva* is never found in the transitive form. The English language does a good job of giving a sense of the Sanskrit: as a fire "goes out" or "is extinguished" for lack of fuel, so also the false view of the self simply "goes out." There is no self that has extinguished this false view. Paradoxically, there is the extinguishing of the illusion, but no "one" who has done the extinguishing.

Not surprisingly, the metaphor of a lamp flame going out is a very common image for nirvana in early Buddhist literature. The story of Patacara is a fine example of the lamp-flame metaphor. The story begins with Patacara as a young woman who recklessly takes a lover and flees her family only to lose every-thing—children, lover, parents—before converting to Buddhism and becoming a nun. As a nun Patacara's life is not easy either. At one point in her story she looks out from her monastery and is afflicted with a longing and despair that all monks and nuns, whether Buddhist or Christian, will recognize:

> Ploughing the fields, sowing seeds in the earth, men look after their wives and children, and prosper.
>
> Why can't I, who keep the precepts and follow the teachings of the Master, attain nirvana? I am neither lazy nor conceited!
>
> After washing my feet, I note the water, and watch it going down the drain; that makes me collect and control my mind as though it were a noble thoroughbred horse.
>
> Then, taking a lamp, I enter my cell; thinking of going to sleep, I sit down on my bed;
>
> With a pin, I pull out the wick. The lamp goes out: nirvana. My mind is freed.[27]

What is the lamp that goes out? Literally speaking, the nun has removed the wick from the oil lamp burning in her cell. With no more fuel, the lamp goes out. Metaphorically speaking, the lamp is the burning flame of desire that is her mind. This lamp simply goes out. The mind is freed from its obsessions. This is nirvana.

In the story of Patacara, the lamp metaphor actually describes the course of events in which nirvana is realized, not nirvana itself.[28] As a lamp-flame simply goes out, so also our craving and desire is extinguished. The image does not give even a hint as to what nirvana itself might be like. This is because nirvana has something in common with what Christians call the beatific vision, or the vision of God in heaven. No human words can adequately describe nirvana. No human language can capture the experience. The going out of the lamp is part of the world of suffering *(samsara)*. Nirvana is beyond our human experience.

In addition to the image of the extinguishing of a flame, Buddhists sometimes talk about nirvana as the annihilation or the extinction of the illusion of being a separate self. Buddhists are not always as careful about this as they need to be when talking to Christians. Sometimes Buddhists simply say that nirvana is the annihilation of the self. This easily gives the impression that enlightenment entails some kind of self-destruction or suicide. Christians are sometimes left with the idea that Buddhism is pessimistic if not nihilistic. More accurately, nirvana is not about the destruction of the self. Rather, becoming enlightened involves the destruction of the *illusion* of being a self. Is there a self? Is there not a self? Like the Buddha, Buddhists are silent about this metaphysical question. Is there an illusion of being a self? Most certainly there is, and this illusion is nothing but a constellation of desires and cravings that is the origin of suffering. When this illusion is uprooted and destroyed, utterly annihilated and extinguished, *dukkha* ceases.[29]

Some widely recognized Buddhist scholars like to translate nirvana into English as "freedom."[30] More traditionally, the early Buddhist scriptures often refer to nirvana as a realization of truth.[31] The truth that is realized in nirvana is insight into the illusion of the self and insight into how our false views distort our view of the world. With the deconstruction of these false views, there is no longer any compulsion to construct fabrications, no longer a need to cling obsessively to the desirable or flee the abhorrent. And there is no longer a need to deal with the world on the basis of power and anxiety, desire, craving, and obsession. In this respect the truth of nirvana is a radical kind of freedom.

FOURTH NOBLE TRUTH: *MARGA*

For the benefit of his followers the Buddha offered a set of practical teachings known as the eightfold path. This path *(marga)* constitutes the core of the Buddhist life. The Buddha's forty-five years of preaching can be taken as an elaboration of this last of the four Noble Truths:

> And what is the Noble Truth of the way leading to the cessation of suffering? Just this: the Eightfold Noble Path, consisting of right views, right intention, right effort, right action, right livelihood, right speech, right mindfulness, right meditation. This, monks, is the Noble Truth of the way leading to the cessation of suffering.[32]

These eight divisions should not be thought of as sequential steps in an elaborate course of religious development to be followed only by monastics. Instead, they should be thought of as a list of useful practices and guidelines to be adapted and observed by all Buddhists, both lay and monastic, in ways appropriate to their specific religious needs.

Traditionally, the eight injunctions have been bundled into three categories: ethics *(sila)*, mental discipline *(samadhi)*, and wisdom *(prajna)*. Buddhist ethics have to do with right action, right livelihood, and right speech. Buddhist mental discipline consists in right effort, right mindfulness, and right meditation. Buddhist wisdom includes right view and right intention. The counsels of the eightfold path became the basis for the life of the Buddhist community then and today, both monastic and non-monastic. During his forty-five years of preaching the Buddha explained the path to different people in different ways in keeping with their capacity for understanding and practicing. Based on this example from the Buddha himself, Buddhist teachers over the centuries have developed each of the eight divisions with an enormous amount of interpretation and commentary, practical insight and adaptation.

The manifold interpretations of the eightfold path, however important, cannot be explored in any detail here. Suffice it to say that in each of the eight directives the fourth Noble Truth lays down a concrete elaboration of the Buddha's "middle path." The life of the Buddha, as recounted in texts like the "Introduction to the Jatakas," is an example of the wisdom of the middle path. The first part of the Buddha's life was spent in hedonistic self-indulgence behind the high walls of the king's pleasure palace. The second part of the Buddha's life was given over to the opposite extreme, a life of self-denial that almost killed him. Attachment to ascetic practices entails the assertion of the ego and a false view of the self quite as much as attachment to the worldly pleasures that the prince knew in his father's pleasure palace. Taking nourishment from Nandabala, the cow-herder's daughter, Siddhartha began to follow a middle path between these opposites, which led to his eventual enlightenment beneath the banyon tree.

The Buddha's silence before Vacchagotta's questions that do not tend to edification is also an example of taking the middle path. When asked by Vacchagotta if the soul exists, the Buddha's response was silence. When asked if the soul does not exist, the Buddha's response was silence. An affirmative reply to either question would not be the truth. But neither would a negative response be true to the Buddha's right view. The Buddha's silence cannot be construed as a negative response to either of Vacchagotta's questions. The right view, according to Buddhism, is to avoid attachment to either those who hold for the existence of a soul or those who deny its existence. This is the middle path of the Buddha: the silence that is non-attachment.

3

The Mind on Fire

Nowhere is the Buddha's insight into the depths of desire more apparent than in his famous "Fire Sermon." The Buddha had been staying in Uruvela before moving to Gaya, both in northeast India. At Gaya he assembled his followers and began to preach to them as follows:

> All things, O priests, are on fire. And what, O priests, are all these things which are on fire?
> The eye, O priests, is on fire; forms are on fire; . . . impressions received by the eye are on fire; and whatever sensation, pleasant, unpleasant or indifferent . . . that also is on fire.
> And with what are these on fire?
> With the fire of passion, I say, with the fire of hatred, with the fire of infatuation; with birth, old age, death, sorrow, lamentation, misery, grief, and despair they are on fire.

But the Buddha does not limit this conflagration to the eye. The sermon continues by claiming,

> The ear is on fire; sounds are on fire... the nose is on fire; odors are on fire; . . . the tongue is on fire; tastes are on fire; . . . the body is on fire; things tangible are on fire; . . . the mind is on fire; ideas are on fire.[1]

Even the mind itself is on fire, with passion and hatred to be sure, but the mind is also feverish with "infatuation; with birth, old age, death, sorrow, lamentation, misery, grief, and despair." And what fuels this fire? Not only sensations, pleasant, unpleasant or indifferent, but ideas stoke the flames of the fire that consumes the mind.

The school of thought founded by Nagarjuna is called Madhyamika, a name that means the "philosophy of the middle path." To this extent, at least, it is plain that Nagarjuna's intent was to capture in philosophy the religious insight of the Buddha's teaching. But in what sense is it possible to capture the Buddha's teaching with philosophical ideas? Will not this effort merely throw more fuel onto the fire of the mind? In a strictly religious sense the Buddha's middle path is a matter of practicing non-attachment by avoiding extremes of self-indulgence and self-denial. Intellectually speaking, the middle path of the Buddha is a matter of non-attachment to conceptual extremes. Take, for example, the following text selected from the Sutras.

The background to this dialogue between the Buddha and a certain Kaccayana is identical to that of the story of the Buddha's silence, namely, the debate between the eternalists and the annihilationists. The eternalists held that there was an eternal Self or soul (*atman*) that was ultimately identical with the everlasting and unchanging metaphysical foundation of the universe (Brahman). On the other hand, the annihilationists, or nihilists, denied the existence of such an eternal Self as well as the existence of a metaphysical foundation to all things. In doing so, they also denied the existence of any basis for moral behavior. The story is told by Ananda, one of the Buddha's original disciples:

> Thus have I heard: The Blessed One was once living at Savatthi in the monastery of Anathapindika, in Jeta's Grove. At that time, the venerable Kaccayana of that clan came to visit him, and saluting him, sat down at one side. So seated, he questioned the Exalted one: "Sir, [people] speak of 'right view, right view.' To what extent is there a right view?"

And the Buddha answered the monk as follows:

> This world, Kaccayana, is generally inclined towards two [views]: existence and non-existence. To him who perceives with right wisdom the uprising of the world as it has come to be, the notion of non-existence in the world does not occur. Kaccayana, to him who perceives with right wisdom the ceasing of the world as it has come to be, the notion of existence in the world does not occur. . . .
>
> "Everything exists"—this, Kaccayana, is one extreme. "Everything does not exist"—this, Kaccayana, is the second extreme.
>
> Kaccayana, without approaching either extreme, the *Tathagata* [the Buddha] teaches you a doctrine by the middle.[2]

The unenlightened mind is forced into choosing between two mutually exclusive ideas: either there is an absolute foundation to reality, such as Brahman or Being Itself or God, or there is no such thing at all and no basis for either the religious quest or for morality. But for the enlightened one, neither of these two extreme alternatives is a helpful path to take. The one who is awakened clings neither to one extreme nor the other. This is the middle path.

For present purposes, the question that initiates the conversation between the Buddha and Kaccayana is more important than the Buddha's answer. "Right view, right view—to what extent is there a right view?" It is not a right view to claim that all exists by arising out of a metaphysical absolute. Simultaneously, it is not a right view to claim the opposite. Therefore, in order to maintain a right view of the universe and all that is within it, it would seem that the best course would be to forsake philosophy altogether and revert to the silence of the Buddha.

Madhyamika thinkers, including Nagarjuna, were keenly aware of the difficulties entailed in trying to capture in ideas the religious insight of the Buddha. If
ideas keep the mind aflame, is not the wisest course to forsake ideas altogether?
How does one capture the meaning of the Buddha's silence using philosophical
concepts? In order to do so, the Madhyamika philosophers developed what Buddhists in Japan have called a philosophy that is not a philosophy.[3] That is, a
philosophy that does not hold up a philosophical position among others as true
and absolute, but rather a philosophy that leads us on a quest for truth that is in
fact the Buddha's middle path of enlightenment through non-attachment. The
word *madyamika* itself, which can be translated "middlemost,"[4] indicates that
Nagarjuna and his followers developed a peculiar way of doing philosophy that
charts a middle path between the twin conceptual extremes of eternalism and
annihilationism, both of which the Buddha taught his disciples to renounce. The
point of such a philosophy is not to frustrate the mind with the absurdity of life
and the utter failure of reason to lead us to wisdom. Rather, Nagarjuna taught his
disciples to use philosophy as a tool in the Buddhist religious quest to eradicate
our obsessions at their root and, in this manner, to follow the Buddha along the
middle path.

NAGARJUNA

What can be known with historical reliability about the life and teaching activity of Nagarjuna is scant indeed. So highly did subsequent generations vener-
ate Nagarjuna's thought that he has been elevated by some to the status of a
"second Buddha," and on occasion his name has been affixed fraudulently to
documents in order to bestow on them an incontestable authority.[5] Adulation
such as this has only increased the difficulty of determining historically reliable
facts about his life. There is, however, scholarly consensus regarding the fact that
Nagarjuna was born into a Brahmin family in South India and became influential
as a thinker around the year AD 150, roughly seven centuries after the life of
Siddhartha Gautama. His fame seems to have spread from the south of India
northwestward into the Gandhara area in the far north. There is a Tibetan tradition that holds that he was a student of Rahulabhadra, but other traditions, both
Tibetan and Chinese and probably more reliable, hold that Rahulabhadra was a
student of Nagarjuna.[6] He may have taught at the prestigious Buddhist monastic
university of Nalanda. Nagarjuna is the founder of Buddhism's Madhyamika
school. Within the school, Nagarjuna's followers include Aryadeva (170–270),
Buddhapalita (470–540), Bhavaviveka (490–570), Candrakirti (600–650), and
Santideva (650–750).[7]

One way to measure this monk's importance for the Buddhist tradition is to
note that Nagarjuna is revered as a patriarch by almost all the various branches of
Mahayana Buddhism (Chinese, Korean, Japanese, and Vietnamese) and Vajrayana
Buddhism (Tibetan and Mongolian). In time, his fame spread from India to China
by way of Central Asia through the capable work of the great translator and

commentator Kumarajiva, who came to China from Central Asia around the year 402.[8] Nagarjuna's thought became widely influential in Tibet and Mongolia through the commentaries of Candrakirti (c. 600–650). The lack of historical knowledge is partly due to the fact that he has been such a commanding figure in the history of Buddhism. As his prestige among Buddhists began to grow, legends about Nagarjuna's extraordinary religious achievements and superhuman powers as an alchemist began to arise.[9]

Nagarjuna's wide influence should serve notice that his thought encapsulates something that rings true to Buddhists of many different times, places, and languages. But it also should alert us to a wide range of differing interpretations of his work. One measure of the fidelity of Nagarjuna's thought to the inspiration of the Buddha is the fact that he has been misunderstood in ways very similar to the ways the Buddha has been misunderstood. In the last hundred years Nagarjuna's Madhyamika philosophy has been described erroneously as nihilism, irrationalism, agnosticism, monism, skepticism, mysticism, and relativism.[10] There is a small library of works by Asian and Western scholars, ancient and modern, that interpret and comment on the *Stanzas*. Nagarjuna's most influential contemporary interpreters include Frederick Streng, Kenneth Inada, Paul Williams, David Ruegg, Christian Lindtner (all of whose research has been influential in the West), and Gadjin Nagao (whose work has been widely influential in Japan).[11] Most Buddhist scholars have seen Nagarjuna as an early representative of the Mahayana branch of Buddhism and thus an innovator within the developing Buddhist intellectual tradition. This general consensus of scholars tends to emphasize the continuity of Nagarjuna's thought with later developments in the Buddhism of China, Korea and Japan. In contrast to this line of interpretation, David Kalupahana takes a more controversial position, arguing that Nagarjuna is not a Mahayana figure and indeed is more of a commentator on the early tradition than an innovator, one who sought to return Buddhist thinking to the original teachings of the historical Buddha. In Japan, Gadjin Nagao's reading of Nagarjuna has been significantly shaped by the Tibetan commentaries on his works.[12]

With such a diversity of views about the meaning of Nagarjuna's thought, the most sensible approach for comparative theology should be to rely on the consensus that exists among scholars and to bring the conflicts that separate them into the discussion where it is useful to do so. In taking this approach I am following the advice of some of my own Buddhist teachers and companions in dialogue, especially Professor Masao Abe and the Venerable Havanpola Ratanasara. This chapter, in particular, will concentrate on the consensus. In the chapters to follow, in which Nagarjuna's philosophy of emptiness will be compared with Aquinas's understanding of how it is that God remains incomprehensible to human beings, the conflict of interpretations regarding Nagarjuna will prove useful in exploring and revising our understanding of the Christian doctrine of God. Regardless of how controversial his interpretation of Nagarjuna might be, David Kalupahana's translation and commentary of the *Stanzas* cannot be ignored, and his translation will be used throughout.

AFTER THE BUDDHA

In a dialogue session with Christians, Nishitani Keiji, one of the great Japanese Buddhist thinkers of the twentieth century, noted that religions are "living things."[13] No religion ever stands still. Like all living things, religions are constantly interacting with their environment. After the time of Christ, for example, Christianity was increasingly required to explain itself to the Greco-Roman world. In doing so, Christians made use of Greek thought to articulate many of its most basic teachings. Christian theological terms like *Holy Trinity* and *incarnation* do not appear as such in the New Testament. These doctrines entered the Christian theological lexicon by means of a long process of using Greek philosophical concepts to clarify the meaning of the scriptures and the belief of the worshiping Christian community.

For Indian Buddhism, interacting with the social environment meant understanding itself in relation to the great river of religious creativity that is India itself. In the days of the historical Buddha and after, India was buzzing with myriad schools of thought and devotional movements. In order better to understand Nagarjuna and the *Stanzas*, it will be helpful to look at two elements of the development of the Buddhist tradition after the time of Siddhartha, the Abhidharma philosophy and Mahayana Buddhism's new understanding of the Buddha.

One particular challenge and opportunity India presented to the Buddhist community was a love of devotional religion *(bhakti)* and philosophical belief in an Ultimate Reality (Brahman) and an eternal Self *(atman)*. Buddhists responded to the challenge to explain itself to India with an energetic defense of Siddhartha's basic teachings that not even the Golden Age of Buddhism in T'ang Dynasty China was able to match for its creativity and energy.[14] Instead of simply retelling the stories of the Buddha's dialogues and discourses in the Sutras, the monks began to elaborate and explain the Buddha's teaching with philosophical arguments. These tracts were eventually collected into a body of literature known as the Abhidharma. Although the Abhidharma is more theoretical than the sermons and dialogues in the Sutras, the purpose lying behind this effort remained the Buddhists' religious effort to eliminate false assumptions about the self and experience that promoted attachment and the thirst for further existence.

In the Abhidharma the monks attempted to define and classify all the various factors *(dharmas)* that are constantly combining in countless ways to form everyday experience. In this way the Abhidharma can be seen as an elaboration on the early Buddhist teaching regarding the five aggregates *(skandhas)* that we see in the Sutras. To this end the Abhidharma movement developed various systems of thought for factoring ordinary experience into complex classifications of *dharmas* and their interrelationships.[15] To the aggregates *(skandhas)* were added the six senses *(indriya)*, their respective objects *(visaya)*, and an enormous taxonomy of mental states *(cetasika)*. In accord with the theory of dependent arising *(pratitya-samutpada)*, the *dharmas* are constantly arising in the form of a specific state of mind, enduring for a moment, and then dissolving into component parts before arising again momentarily as a new state of mind. Armed with these conceptual tools, the Abhidharma analysts were able to develop various systems to account for mental states and false views, for explaining how the illusory sense of being a separate self arises, and for discerning the various stages of spiritual progress.

Attachment to the world is driven by the mind's propensity to shape experience into false views *(maccha-ditthi)* such that our desire-driven illusions about the world are taken as absolutely real and no longer as fabrications generated by the mind's thirst for further existence. Attachments generated by our false views are the origin of suffering. By analyzing our false views into their component parts, the Abhidharma philosophers tried to show that what seems so undeniably real (and thus either desirable or repulsive) is in fact a passing illusion that has been momentarily constructed and, in fact, will momentarily be deconstructed by the flux and flow of reality. By gaining insight into how illusions arise, attachment to these illusions ceases and suffering is overcome. In their effort to understand the arising of false views, the Abhidharma thinkers generally took a realistic approach to the *dharmas*. Unlike our illusions, the *dharmas* have an "inherent existence" *(svabhava)* and are real in an objective sense. This being the case, it was easy for the Abhidharma philosophers to take the next step in arguing that since the *dharmas* are real, their theories about the *dharmas* likewise have an objective truth.

The second major development to be addressed is the rise of Mahayana Buddhism in India. Early Buddhism was a religion of monks and nuns, not particularly well suited for farmers, merchants, or anyone else unable or disinclined to enter a monastery. What about the needs of lay people? Within a few hundred years after the Buddha, a movement within Buddhism more suited to the religious needs of lay people began to grow in influence and popularity. This is the Buddhism of the Greater Vehicle, or Mahayana.

Mahayana Buddhists began to revere the historical Buddha as an object of devotion *(bhakti)*, partially in response to the immense popularity of this way of being religious in India. The historical figure, Siddhartha Gautama, gradually took on the status of a cosmic savior. This process was propelled not only by the religious needs of ordinary people but also by an ambiguity about the Buddha that was part of the tradition from its earliest stages. For example, in reply to a priest's question about his identity, the Buddha declared himself to be neither a god nor a human being, but rather an "enlightened one" *(Buddha)*, leaving unclarified what exactly a Buddha is, if neither a god nor a human being. "Like the beautiful lotus which is unsmeared by water, even so am I untainted by the world. Hence . . . I am a Buddha."[16] In addition, monks entering the religious life would publicly announce that they had taken "refuge" in not only the Buddha's teaching and the monastic community but also in the Buddha himself. Ambiguities such as these left the tradition open to much innovation.

As the historical Buddha gradually came to be venerated as a savior figure, traditions regarding the existence of previous Buddhas began to gain in popularity. Siddhartha Gautama came to be seen as the Buddha of this particular historical era, one of countless Buddhas who have come to save human beings eon after eon into the infinite past. Alongside these traditions there arose belief in Maitreya, the Buddha of the era to come. Eventually, Mahayana Buddhists began to envision an elaborate universe full of savior Buddhas. For example, there is Avalokitesvara, known as Guan-yin in China and Kannon in Japan, the personification of infinite compassion. There is also Amitabha, Amitofo in China and Amida in Japan, who has vowed to save all who call on him. There is also Ksitigarbha, Japan's Jizo, who saves all from falling into hell and who, in Japan at least, is especially compassionate toward children.

The intellectual achievements of the Abhidharma philosophers and the religious popularity of the Mahayana movement were not without risk for the Buddhist tradition. The goal of the Abhidharma analysts was to preserve the Buddha's original insight into reality as the dependent arising of all *dharmas*. Thus the intention of the Abhidharma school, at least originally, was to support the monk's quest for enlightenment, not philosophical speculation for its own sake. The Abhidharma movement, however, also ran the considerable risk of becoming merely another academic approach to problems in metaphysics that had become disengaged from the religious practice of the Buddhist community. Like eternalism and annihilationism, the Abhidharma movement's assertions about the reality of the *dharmas* could easily be counted as another "idea on fire" fueling the passions of the mind. As such, the Abhidharma would not measure up to the religious insight of the Buddha's middle path through opposing views. Similarly, Mahayana Buddhism, with its belief in savior Buddhas, ran the risk of falling away from the authentic tradition. If the cosmic Buddha is more exalted than the myriad gods, should we think of the Buddha as a supreme being or as God beyond the gods? As with the problem of the Abhidharma philosophy, the Buddhist community's devotion to the savior Buddhas ran the risk of betraying the Buddha's silence about God and straying from the middle path by allowing the cosmic Buddha to become objectivized within the mind as an object to be desired. Even the Buddha can become a "false view" to which the mind can become attached, if not obsessed and ultimately inflamed.

In a body of writings known collectively as the "Perfection of Wisdom" literature *(Prajna-paramita)*, we can see the beginnings of a response to these problems. Starting about a century before the birth of Nagarjuna, hymns and Sutras (ascribed to the historical Buddha) began to appear urging Buddhists to seek the perfection of wisdom by realizing in their lives the ultimate emptiness of all things. Among these writings is the famous Heart Sutra, wherein the Buddha teaches his disciple Sariputra the following:

> The bodhisattva, the Noble Avalokitesvara [Guan-yin or Kannon], while carrying out his practice in profound transcendent wisdom, contemplated the five aggregates *(skandhas)* and he saw that they were empty of inherent self-existence *(svabhava)*.
>
> Here, O Sariputra, form is emptiness and emptiness is form. Form is not other than emptiness, and emptiness not other than form; whatever is form, that is emptiness, and whatever is emptiness, that is form. So it is also for [the four other aggregates].[17]

These lines contain within them a direct criticism of the Abhidharma's realistic view of the *dharmas*. "Form" is one of the *skandhas* that make up the illusion of the self and thus also one of the *dharmas*. In contrast to the traditional Abhidharma teaching, form is not seen to be real in itself. It has no "inherent self-existence" *(svabhava)*. Like the illusion of being an eternal self *(atman)*, even the five *skandhas* are illusory and come into being like everything else through the process of dependent arising *(pratitya-samutpada)*. Form is empty, that is, lacking in any permanent, substantial quality.

In claiming that form is emptiness, the Heart Sutra, and the Perfection of Wisdom literature in general, holds that it is not only our false views about the world that are illusory. The *dharmas* are too. Herein can be found the makings of a revolution in Buddhist thinking. If the *dharma*, quite as much as the illusions they generate, are not substantial realities, then even the concepts, the distinctions, the systems, and the theories constructed by the Abhidharma scholars with their elaborate analyses of experience are not to be taken as literally true either. In fairness, it should be repeated that the intent of the Abhidharma was to aid the monks in discerning the nature of their illusions with the hope of overcoming them in the quest for enlightenment. However, the danger of the Buddha's middle path decaying into yet another theoretical view of reality, like eternalism or annihilationism, should not be dismissed lightly.

The Heart Sutra's famous admonition that "form is emptiness and emptiness is form" is more than a criticism of the Abhidharma theorists. The Buddha, cosmically enthroned as a savior figure, is also a "form" fabricated by the mind. The great savior Buddhas, Avalokitesvara, Ksitigarbha and Amitabha as well as Maitreya, the Buddha to come, quite as much as the illusion of the permanent self, can arise in the mind as an "idea on fire." Thus even the Buddha, considered as a form appearing within consciousness as a benevolent savior figure, should be thought of as thoroughly empty. If wisdom leads one to a devotional faith in the savior Buddhas, then the perfection of wisdom leads one to the realization that even the Buddhas, to the extent that they become objects of desire, are illusions to which we must stop clinging if we are to find release from suffering. This is not to say that the Perfection of Wisdom literature calls for the veneration of the Buddhas to stop. It suggests, rather, that the cosmic Buddha's deepest reality is not that of the Christian God who creates and sustains the world, the God who can exist apart from the world and is in no way dependent on the world. Rather, the form that is venerated is itself utterly empty and without inherent self-existence *(svabhava)*. In realizing this emptiness, the Buddhist perfects wisdom by becoming free even of attachment to the Buddha.

The Abhidharma and the Perfection of Wisdom literature are in agreement on one weighty matter: enlightenment is to be found by apprehending reality correctly. But there are significant differences that distinguish them as well. The Abhidharma seeks to overcome false views by defining, analyzing, and cataloguing the numerous factors *(dharmas)* with which the mind constructs illusions. The Perfection of Wisdom literature seeks the "right view" of reality in the nullification of all the mind's theoretical constructions by asserting the emptiness of all.

Nagarjuna was the heir to both of these traditions within Buddhism. From the Abhidharma scholars he derived a sense of the skillful use of logical analysis as a means to guide the mind to be freed of its obsessions. From the Perfection of Wisdom literature he gained an insight of the emptiness of all.

MADHYAMIKA PHILOSOPHY

A book should be counted a classic not because of the layers of dust it has managed to accumulate on its shelf by remaining unread for so many years, but rather the opposite. Books we find ourselves coming back to again and again, books that present ideas that will not let go of our imagination, are the true classics. It also might be said that books that lead to lively, lasting debates because they ask really good questions about who we are and what we should be doing with our lives can be counted as classics. By any of these standards, Nagarjuna's best-known work, the *Stanzas on the Middle Path (Mulamadhyamakakarika)*,[18] must be counted among the classics of Buddhist literature, if not the religious literature of the world. It was originally written in Sanskrit sometime after the year 150. Later it was translated into Chinese and still later into Tibetan and began to influence the development of Buddhism in places like China, Korea, Japan, Vietnam, Tibet, and Mongolia.

At the center of the religious landscape mapped out by Nagarjuna in the *Stanzas* is the Buddhist notion of emptiness *(sunyata)*. Although Nagarjuna is by no means the originator of this idea, the *Stanzas* remains among the classics of Buddhist philosophy concerned with it. In Western civilization the word *emptiness* is easily associated with a bounty of negative associations. Westerners, when confronted with experiences of violence and inhumanity that challenge the basic meaningfulness of life, speak of "that empty feeling." "Empty words" bring forth feelings of disgust or moral indignation. Promises not backed up by deeds ring "hollow" in our ears and breed distrust in our hearts. In India and the other parts of Asia shaped by Buddhist thought, the idea of emptiness has very different connotations.

In the *Stanzas* the Buddhist philosophy of emptiness reached a sophistication and a classic expression that has exerted a considerable force ever since. It makes good sense to divide the entire work into four basic sections.[19] The first section, chapters 1–2, is concerned with the doctrine of dependent arising. In his presentation of the doctrine Nagarjuna does not seem to be concerned with a defense of the basics of traditional Buddhism. There is no discussion, for example, of non-Buddhist arguments against dependent arising. Instead, we find arguments against the Abhidharma belief in the objective reality of the *dharmas*. Nagarjuna's argument relies on the notion of emptiness *(sunyata)* that is so prominent in the Perfection of Wisdom literature. The second section, comprising chapters 3–15, is devoted to a representation of the basic terminology of the Abhidharma philosophers. Nagarjuna's purpose, however, is to show how the *dharmas* should be understood as being empty of objective reality. Chapters 16–26, the third section of the *Stanzas,* have seemed to some readers to be merely a repetition of the material found in the previous chapters. In fact, the ideas developed in these chapters are central to understanding the meaning of emptiness for Nagarjuna. In these chapters Nagarjuna endeavors to show that even teachings as basic to Buddhism as nirvana and the Four Noble Truths are "false views" if allowed to become merely a philosophical viewpoint in opposition to other philosophical theories. The final section (chapter 27) summarizes the work by restating the Buddha's notion of "right view" *(sammâditthi).* Since I am concerned with Nagarjuna's use of the principle of emptiness in the hope of eventually comparing it with Aquinas's understanding of the incomprehensibility of God, I will focus attention on section three (chapters 16–26).

CHAPTER 25: NIRVANA

In chapter 25 of the *Stanzas,* Nagarjuna raises questions about nirvana that a Christian might very well have asked him, given the opportunity. Does nirvana exist as an eternal stillness beyond this changing world of dependent arising? Should nirvana be thought of as a transcendent realm of peace in opposition to the sorrow of *samsara?* Some Christians, had they had the opportunity, might have asked if nirvana was like heaven, a place we go to after we die (although this would betray a somewhat naive view of what Christians mean by heaven). A more Buddhist way of stating the problem would be to ask questions like the following: Is nirvana an escape from *samsara?* Does nirvana lie beyond this world of suffering? Is nirvana the opposite of *samsara?* Is nirvana *something* to be desired? Posing questions such as these makes it easier to understand the danger Nagarjuna saw inherent in any attempt to capture the religious insight of the Buddha using static concepts. To the extent that we think of nirvana as a place (a transcendent realm beyond *samsara)* or a state of being (eternal bliss as opposed to the sorrow of this world), nirvana ends up becoming an object within our minds. Conceptualizing nirvana into a mental object supplies more fuel to the fire of our minds. Then nirvana becomes an object of desire, the source of sorrow. Somewhat paradoxically, to the extent that nirvana is conceived of as something to be desired, it is not nirvana at all, but rather just another part of the flux and flow of *samsara.* Monks would be well advised to stop thinking about nirvana.

How might we avoid this "false view" of nirvana? Should we talk about nirvana in terms of "existence" or its opposite, "nonexistence"? To talk about nirvana in terms of existence would be to claim that nirvana exists as a book or a table exists. This is misleading. Books and tables come into being and inevitably perish within the realm of *samsara.* Nirvana does not exist as a dependently arisen object within *samsara.* To say that nirvana does not exist is equally misleading. If it does not exist, how can there be any release from suffering as the Buddha taught in the third Noble Truth? In seeking to avoid all false views about nirvana, Nagarjuna makes four basic statements, all of which, it should be well noted, are denials:

Freedom [nirvana], as a matter of fact, is not existence, for if it were, it would follow that it has the characteristic of decay and death. Indeed, there is no existence without decay and death.

If freedom is not existence, will freedom be non-existence? Wherein there is no existence, therein non-existence is not evident.

If freedom were to be both existence and non-existence, then release would also be both existence and non-existence. This too is not proper.

The proposition that freedom is neither existence nor non-existence could be established if and when both existence and non-existence are established.[20]

Nagarjuna's fourfold negation (the *catuskoti*) has been carefully constructed in order to exclude logically all possible metaphysical views about the existence and nonexistence of nirvana. Nagarjuna's view of nirvana is *not* any of the following:

1. Nirvana exists,
2. Nirvana does not exist,
3. Nirvana both exists and does not exist, and
4. Nirvana neither exists nor does not exist.

Thinking of nirvana as a transcendental state of being beyond this world is not a right view conducive to finding release from suffering. And the same can be said about the opposite position. Thinking of nirvana as a state of utter annihilation, the nothingness that results from the destruction of existence, is not a right view of nirvana either. Such an understanding of nirvana is not conducive to finding release from suffering. As a philosophical concept, nirvana is a distraction from the middle path that leads to freedom. Those who are obsessed with it are attached to an idea that keeps the mind burning. In fact, nirvana is completely empty.

In these four negations Nagarjuna is not rejecting the preaching of the Buddha. Rather, he is rejecting any attempt to fix this preaching in static concepts. Even a Buddhist doctrine as basic as nirvana becomes a false view when objectified as simply another philosophical position. Therefore, in the attempt to express the wisdom of the Buddha philosophically, Nagarjuna saw that the most appropriate use of logic was to use it to clarify all possible false views without asserting an alternative right view. Such a course is the most appropriate because nirvana is empty of any substance or inherent self-existence *(svabhava)*. It is not a goal to be attained, a metaphysical realm that can be contrasted with *samsara*, a heaven beyond this earth. Those who are attached to the concept of nirvana are by that very fact prevented from realizing nirvana in their lives. Likewise, those who claim that there is no nirvana, against those who claim there is, have not realized a right view of the world. As a concept, nirvana is a mental fabrication that arises dependently along with all our other mental fabrications. Wisdom comes in overcoming all false views of nirvana that would suggest otherwise.

THE TATHAGATA

Of all the titles bestowed on the Buddha by his disciples, none of them held as much potential for misunderstanding as the title "Tathagata." Buddhists do not speak of the Buddha's "death" but rather his *parinirvana*, the continuation of his enlightenment without a body. Tathagata ("thus come, thus gone") is the title bestowed on the Buddha to indicate his paradoxical status after the *parinirvana*. Does the enlightened one exist eternally after death or is *parinirvana* to be thought of as the utter annihilation of individuality? If the former is the case, then the Tathagata would become in fact a metaphysical self, the eternal soul *(atman)*, which is not in keeping with Buddhist teaching. If the latter is the case, then the *parinirvana* becomes a death, the utter destruction of selfhood.

One way to think about the status of the Tathagata is to use Abhidharma philosophical analysis. In the realm of *samsara*, all things arise in the form of momentary configurations of the aggregates *(skandhas)*. This includes the body of the Buddha. After eighty years the body simply came apart, while the enlightenment continued. What about the Buddha's enlightenment? Does the Tathagata (in effect, the Buddha's enlightenment) arise in terms of the dependent arising of aggregates? If this were the case, the Tathagata would be in *samsara*, not nirvana. If the Tathagata exists apart from the process of dependent arising, then the Tathagata would seem to be a kind of Supreme Being or eternal self *(atman)*. Is the Tathagata no different than the aggregates or does the Tathagata exist apart from them? Chapter 22 of the *Stanzas* begins with the following statement:

> The *tathagata* is neither the aggregates nor different from them. The aggregates are not in him; nor is he in the aggregates. He is not possessed of the aggregates. In such a context, who is a *tathagata*?[21]

If the Tathagata can neither be identified with nor distinguished from the aggregates, then in order to maintain a right view of the Buddha after the *parinirvana*, one must rule out thinking of the Tathagata either as an eternal self *(atman)* or as the utter destruction of individual identity.

The problem of achieving a right view of the Tathagata can also be placed in the context of Mahayana Buddhist devotion to the savior Buddhas. Enlightenment frees one from the karmic chains that bind us to the great cycles of death and rebirth that constitute *samsara*. This being the case, should an enlightened one be thought of as immortal? Does the Buddha, after the *parinirvana*, become an eternal Self, existing beyond the sting of death and rebirth? If the *parinirvana* did not transform the Buddha into an eternal Self, did it utterly obliterate any sense of selfhood whatsoever?

These questions are reminiscent of the story of the Buddha's silence before the "indeterminate questions." In choosing the title Tathagata, the early Buddhist community was trying to practice the middle path of renouncing both eternalism and annihilationism. In his treatment of the status of the Tathagata, Nagarjuna wants to preserve this insight by having recourse to the same fourfold negation he used in his discussion of nirvana:

It is not assumed that the Blessed One [Tathagata] exists after death.
Neither is it assumed that he does not exist, or both or neither.[22]

Nagarjuna advises his followers to renounce all possible false views of the
Tathagata. Existence, nonexistence, both, neither: to become attached to any or
all of these positions would be to become embroiled in conceptual views of the
Tathagata that are not in keeping with the Buddha's middle path and not helpful
in finding release from suffering. In fact, to have any one of these false views of
the Tathagata is to fail to perceive the Tathagata and to be blinded by attachments
to *samsara*:

> Those who generate obsessions with great regard to the Buddha who has
> gone beyond obsessions and is constant, all of them, impaired by obses-
> sions, do not perceive the *Tathagata*.[23]

Here, Nagarjuna the teacher is offering practical advice to his monastic students.
Devotion to the Buddha, however pious it may seem externally, can become a
snare that is harmful to the Buddhist religious life for a monk.

Like nirvana, the Tathagata is not to be thought of as existing or not existing.
The Tathagata is not to be thought of as a supernatural being. To think so is to
suffer from a false view. Likewise, the Tathagata is not to be thought of as the
sheer annihilation of individual existence. To think so is also a false view. The
right view of the Buddha after *parinirvana* is to recognize that the Tathagata is
"empty" of both existence and nonexistence.

THE DISCOURSE TO VACCHAGOTTA

The roots of Nagarjuna's philosophical way of deconstructing philosophical
views become evident when we compare this section of the *Stanzas* with a passage from one of the Sutras. In the "Discourse to Vacchagotta on Fire" the wandering monk Vacchagotta asks the Buddha about the status of the Tathagata.
Once again, in Buddhist tradition, the disciple Ananda tells the story:

> Thus have I heard: At one time the Lord was staying near Savatthi in the
> Jeta Grove. . . . Then the wanderer Vacchagotta approached the Lord; hav-
> ing approached, he exchanged greetings with the Lord; having conversed
> in a friendly and courteous way, he sat down at a respectful distance. As he
> was sitting down at a respectful distance, the wanderer Vacchagotta spoke
> thus to the Lord . . .

A dialogue on several topics ensues. The Buddha carefully responds to each of
Vacchagotta's questions. First, Vacchagotta asks the Buddha a series of questions related to his views about the eternity of the world. This is followed by
another series of questions and answers regarding the relationship between the
soul and the body. The third topic on Vacchagotta's mind is the status of the
Tathagata after death:

Now, good Gotama, is the revered Gotama [the Buddha] of this view: "The Tathagata is after dying, this is indeed the truth, all else is falsehood?"

I, Vaccha, am not of this view: "The Tathagata is after dying, this is indeed the truth, all else is falsehood."

Then, good Gotama, is the revered Gotama of this view: "The Tathagata is not after dying, this is indeed the truth, all else is falsehood?"

I, Vaccha, am not of this view: "The Tathagata is not after dying, this is indeed the truth, all else is falsehood."

Now, good Gotama, is the revered Gotama of this view: "The Tathagata both is and is not after dying, this is indeed the truth, all else is falsehood?"

I, Vaccha, am not of this view: "The Tathagata both is and is not after dying, this is indeed the truth, all else is falsehood."

Then, good Gotama, is the revered Gotama of this view: "The Tathagata neither is nor is not after dying, this is indeed the truth, all else is false-hood?"

I, Vaccha, am not of this view: "The Tathagata neither is nor is not after dying, this is indeed the truth, all else is falsehood."[24]

The conversation recorded in the Sutra is not at all spontaneous or improvised. Both the questions posed by Vacchagotta and the responses given by the Buddha have been carefully choreographed into its present form. The propositions Vacchagotta poses to the Buddha regarding the Tathagata are carefully organized to cover every possible speculative position the mind might generate. These propositions, none of which is the Buddha's view, might be schematized as follows:

A *is* B
A *is not* B
A *is and is not* B
A *is not* (*is and is not* B)

Propositions one and two are straightforward. The first is a simple affirmation, the second a simple negation. The first proposition asserts that the Tathagata exists after death. Were the Buddha to affirm this proposition, Vacchagotta might rightly be led to conclude that the Tathagata is some sort of eternal Self that exists in nirvana as a kind of "heaven" beyond *samsara*. This, of course, is not the Buddha's teaching. Such a false view of the Tathagata does not extinguish the fires of the mind, for it does not lead to the ending of attachment. The second proposition asserts that the Tathagata does not exist after death. Were the Buddha to affirm such a position, Vacchagotta might rightly be led to conclude that enlightenment entails the complete annihilation of our individuality. Neither is this the teaching of the Buddha, for neither annihilationism nor eternalism is conducive to bringing about an end to suffering.

Proposition three, however, is considerably more complicated. This position has to be included among the propositions Vacchagotta poses to the Buddha because it raises a possibility not envisioned by either the first or the second proposition. This proposition states that the Tathagata both exists and does not exist after death. Here we have neither an affirmation nor a negation, simply speaking, but to think of proposition three as an attempt to confront the mind with a logical contradiction would be a mistake. The proposition does not claim that the Tathagata exists after death and at the same time, in an utterly contradictory way, does not exist after death. Instead, proposition three offers us a third possibility. Proposition three might be read, "In one respect the Tathagata exists after death and in another respect the Tathagata does not exist."

Christians should feel right at home here, for this is a common way their tradition has of speaking about God using analogies. For example, most Christians would feel comfortable singing of God as "a mighty fortress," but without presuming that this is literally so. God utterly surpasses every finite way we have of imagining God. On the one hand, the world offers the Christian imagination an abundance of images that serve as splendid analogies for God. On the other hand, none of these images is anything more than analogy; the images do not come close to exhausting the transcendent mystery to which they point. God is like a mighty fortress and also like the father of a prodigal son. God is like innumerable things that exist. And at the same time, God is utterly unlike anything that exists.

Does the Tathagata exist after death or not? One position to take would be yes (proposition one). Another possible position to take would be no (proposition two). A third possible answer would be to say that the status of the Tathagata after death is considerably more complex than either one of these simple positions can handle. Does the Tathagata both exist and not exist? And, of course, the Buddha carefully denies that this more complex position is his view. Were he to identify himself with this both/and position, Vacchagotta might be led to believe that the Tathagata is like the transcendent Mystery of which some of the Christian mystics have sung, or the Absolute One of the neo-Platonist thinkers. In both of these cases a transcendent Absolute is connected with the ordinary world in such a way that analogies, although ultimately inadequate, are nevertheless possible. According to the Buddha, this position is not helpful in finding release from suffering either, and he advises that it be renounced.

Proposition four, like proposition three, is also more complicated than the first two. Logically speaking, proposition four negates what proposition three affirms. Instead of both existing and not existing, proposition four asserts that the Tathagata neither exists nor does not exist after death. This fourth possibility has to be included among the positions Vacchagotta poses to the Buddha because it is a possibility not covered by any of the three foregoing propositions. Like proposition three, this fourth position does not confront the mind with a logical contradiction. Also like proposition three, proposition four implies that thinking in terms of existence or nonexistence is wholly inadequate to the task of understanding what the Tathagata is like. But where proposition three offers us a both/and, proposition four suggests a neither/nor.

Once again, after a little reflection, Christians will decipher patterns of thought recognizable within their own tradition. Not only do Christians talk about what God *is* by using analogies, but they also talk about what God *is not* by using negations. This latter way of knowing God is also prominently featured in Christian

mystical literature. John of the Cross, for instance, is famous for his insistence
that God is *Nada* (nothing). John of the Cross, of course, is a mystic, not a nihil-
ist. The nothingness of God results from the fact that all our analogies ultimately
fail to capture the divine essence. God is "not this and not that." Mystics like
John feel quite comfortable with the idea that the Divine is revealed not only by
affirming what God is like (the cataphatic path), but all the more so by affirming
what God is not like (the apophatic path).

Does the Tathagata exist after death or not? Yes? No? Both? A fourth position
would be to say that the status of the Tathagata is such that neither existence nor
nonexistence adequately fits the bill. And, of course, the Buddha denies that this
relatively more sophisticated position is his view. Were he to affirm this position,
Vacchagotta might be led to believe that after death the Tathagata becomes a
kind of ineffable Absolute that completely transcends the capacity of the human
mind for understanding. Christianity has its own way of negation, but much closer
to home for the Buddha (and for Nagarjuna) was India's own tradition of seeking
the Absolute through negation. For instance, starting in the Hindu Upanishads (c.
800 BC) and continuing in the commentaries which flowed from them, the Absolute (Brahman) was said to be disclosed most profoundly by means of a *neti-
neti* ("not this and not that"). According to the Buddha, neither is this position
adequate for understanding the Tathagata.

Does Nagarjuna's use of this fourfold negation lead us to irrationalism or
even cynicism? After outlining four propositions that cover every possible logical position one might take in trying to understand the nature of nirvana and the
status of the Tathagata after death, Nagarjuna then goes on to show that none of
the four is adequate to the reality in question. In fact, all four are actually harmful. Is Madhyamika philosophy in fact a call to abandon philosophy's quest to
grasp truth with reason? In his own lifetime Nagarjuna was no stranger to the
charge of irrationalism raised by his critics; but where exactly does Nagarjuna
jettison reason? Each proposition is carefully constructed and logically supported
in the *Stanzas*. Far from abandoning reason, it seems much more proper to say
that Nagarjuna is more committed to reason than many other religious thinkers.
Nagarjuna is not promoting irrationalism. Instead, he is asking us to use reason
strategically for a Buddhist purpose. Nagarjuna uses reason in the service of
following the Buddha's middle path of renouncing false views that lead to the
cultivation of sorrow.

In this respect, at least, Nagarjuna shows himself to be an astute student of the
Abhidharma, the Perfection of Wisdom literature, and also a devout Mahayana
Buddhist. As a student of the Abhidharma, Nagarjuna uses reason to clarify what
in fact is a false view of reality. By means of this clarification, attachments to
false views that breed obsessions can be relinquished. The mind is on fire with
ideas that do not lead to release from suffering. Nagarjuna's strategy is to use
reason to remove the fuel that keeps this fire burning. His purpose is not to frustrate the mind with logical absurdities. His purpose is to use logic to identify and
then to rule out every possible speculative view about nirvana and the Tathagata
as metaphysical absolutes to which one might become attached. But Nagarjuna
is also heir to the legacy of the Perfection of Wisdom literature and the notion of

emptiness *(sunyata)*, its great theme. Emptiness, along with logic, is an implement in Nagarjuna's philosophical toolbox, and in order to understand the *Stanzas*, this aspect of Nagarjuna's thought must be explored as well. Finally, Nagarjuna is not merely an academic philosopher, but a devout Mahayana Buddhist. By the strategic use of reason to overcome false views, Nagarjuna "sees" the Tathagata, indeed all the Tathagatas, in their infinite compassion. For all its philosophical sophistication, Nagarjuna's Buddhism is a religion of devotion to the historical Buddha, as well as Avalokitesvara, Amitabha, Ksitigharba, and Maitreya.

THE FETTER OF VIEWS

In the "Discourse to Vacchagotta on Fire," the dialogue between Vacchagotta and the Buddha does not end with the Buddha's rejection of all four of the speculative views regarding the Tathagata we have been examining. At the end of this discussion, Vacchagotta, in some frustration, poses a very pertinent question to the Buddha:

> What is the peril the revered Gotama beholds that he thus does not approach any of these (speculative) views?[25]

And the Buddha responds to Vacchagotta by cautioning him about becoming embroiled in speculative views that breed obsessions and lead to the "thirst for further existence":

> Holding a view, the wilds of views, the wriggling of views, the scuffling of views, the fetter of views; it is accompanied by anguish, distress, misery, fever; it does not conduce to turning away from, nor to dispassion, stopping, calming, super-knowledge, awakening, nor to nibbana [nirvana]. I, Vaccha, beholding that this is a peril, thus do not approach any of these (speculative) views.[26]

Holding a speculative view is not the middle path of the Buddha. Those who stray from this path fall subject not only to "the scuffling of views," but "the fetter of views" as well. That speculative views lead to scuffling is reminiscent of the tradition regarding the Buddha's silence before the indeterminate questions, those speculative issues that seemingly have no answer. But remember that the tradition also refers to these dilemmas as the questions that do not tend to edification. In this respect views lead not only to scuffling but to fetters. Thus, to the extent that faith in the Tathagata and the vision of nirvana can become merely speculative views, even these basic Buddhist doctrines can become the occasion for generating *dukkha*.

Nagarjuna shows his indebtedness to the Perfection of Wisdom literature at the expense of the Abhidharma. According to the Heart Sutra, even the theories of the Abhidharma scholars about the self are empty. The *dharmas* themselves, and not just the illusion of selfhood, have no objective, independent reality *(svabhava)*. All viewpoints *(drsti)* are empty, even our views of the most basic Buddhist doctrines. If we objectify nirvana into a kind of heaven beyond this world, we have strayed from the Buddha's middle path. If we objectify the Tathagata into a kind of transcendent Supreme Being, we have strayed from the Buddha's middle path. Seen as a Supreme Being, the Tathagata is seen falsely. Seen as a transcendent heaven, nirvana is seen falsely. Only by realizing that nirvana and the Tathagata are thoroughly empty can they be seen rightly. False views bind us karmically to *samsara*. Right views free us from the "anguish, distress, misery, and fever" that accompany "holding a view, the wilds of views, the wriggling of views, the scuffling of views, the fetter of views."

If the Tathagata is not a Supreme Being and nirvana is not a transcendent realm beyond this world, then does Nagarjuna want us to think of emptiness itself as the absolute foundation of all? Is emptiness like Aristotle's "prime matter," which can become everything without being anything in particular? Should we conceive of emptiness as an undifferentiated whole out of which the multiplicity of things arises as mere illusion? In the days of the Buddha, as in Nagarjuna's own time, to say nothing of the present, the idea that all things continually arise out of and eventually return to reality's infinite, eternal, and unchanging foundation (Brahman) has been widely accepted in India. Likewise, the Greeks had their own theories about the emanation of all things out of the One. But it would be a mistake to regard emptiness, at least as Nagarjuna uses it in the *Stanzas*, as a metaphysical totality or even as a philosophical concept. To make it into a abstraction like nonexistence is to miss Nagarjuna's point. Most of all, Nagarjuna does not mean to push Buddhism over the cliff of nihilism. Instead, Nagarjuna uses emptiness skillfully as a logical tool for a religious end: prying the mind loose from its attachments to views that fetter us to suffering.

Apparently Nagarjuna was well aware of the danger of making emptiness into a philosophical viewpoint like Brahman or the One of neo-Platonism. As a metaphysical foundation emptiness becomes a philosophical view *(drsti)* not in keeping with the Buddha's middle path. In this regard Nagarjuna offers a number of warnings in the *Stanzas*. For instance, in the thirteenth chapter we find the following passage:

> The Victorious Ones have announced that emptiness is the relinquishing of all views. Those who are possessed of a view of emptiness are said to be incorrigible.[27]

Those who make emptiness into a universal metaphysical foundation for all that appears in the world, indeed, for the universe itself, have taken emptiness and made it a philosophical view, like eternalism or annihilationism. In fact, emptiness is a tool for relinquishing views and nothing more.

Nine chapters later Nagarjuna frankly admits that emptiness itself can become an object of our intellectual obsessions. Becoming attached to even emptiness as a view, however, is an error for which he will accept no blame:

Furthermore, if you were to generate any obsession with regard to emptiness, the accompanying error is not ours. That [obsession] is not appropriate in the context of the empty.[28]

In addition, despite the fact that the term emptiness *(sunyata)* appears everywhere in the *Stanzas*, Nagarjuna never makes the statement "all is empty." Instead, we find statements such as "all *this* is empty."[29] There is no "emptiness itself" beyond the emptiness of particular things. It would be improper to conceive of it as a transcendent reality beyond the world of change *(samsara)* and apart from actual things that are empty.

The *Stanzas* is seasoned generously with verses aimed against Nagarjuna's adversaries. In the twenty-fourth chapter there is also a passage that seems directed more toward his disciples than his opponents. Here we find the famous warning to those who would speculate about emptiness:

> A wrongly perceived emptiness ruins a person of meager intelligence. It is like a snake that is wrongly grasped or knowledge that is wrongly cultivated.[30]

Given the mind's proclivity for generating attachments out of ideas, even ideas like emptiness, speculating about emptiness is dangerous, like grabbing a cobra by the tail instead of its hood. If one is not careful, emptiness can pose a poisonous danger if not handled correctly. Perhaps we might paraphrase Nagarjuna with an image from the Buddha's fire sermon. Playing with emptiness is like playing with fire. If not used carefully, the tool intended to be used for removing fuel from the mind's fire can easily be thrown into the fire as fuel.

In effect, the greatest danger attending Nagarjuna's appeal to emptiness is to forget that emptiness itself is empty and completely bereft of any inherent existence *(svabhava)*. Theorizing about emptiness as if it were the foundation out of which all things appear is to misunderstand completely Nagarjuna's intent. Thus, in regard to the status of the Tathagata, Nagarjuna says:

> "Empty," "non-empty," "both" or "neither"—these should not be declared.
> It is expressed only for the purpose of communication.[31]

The Tathagata should not be conceptualized into a thing that exists or does not exist, for the Tathagata is empty. But neither should the emptiness of the Tathagata become a view. *Emptiness* is merely a term Nagarjuna uses to communicate a religious treaching: those who are faithful to the Buddha's middle path will renounce all their attachments, even their attachments to the Buddha and to the false view of nirvana as an escape from *samsara*.

If Nagarjuna rules out even emptiness as a candidate for giving reality a metaphysical foundation, is his Madhyamika philosophy not a sophisticated form of nihilism? Many of his critics thought so. If nirvana and the Tathagata are empty, so are the Four Noble Truths and the rest of the Buddha's teachings. In fact,

Nagarjuna makes precisely this point in the *Stanzas*.[32] Does this imply that the Buddhist quest for enlightenment and its monastic life is meaninglessness? In Buddhist ordination rites, neophyte monks and nuns take "refuge" in the "three jewels": the Buddha, the monastic community *(samgha)*, and the teachings *(dharma)*. If the three jewels are empty of "inherent existence," what is the point of religious life? In addition, there would seem to be no longer any reason to live a moral life if the "fruits" of action (karma) were without substance. In chapter twenty-four of the *Stanzas*, Nagarjuna sums up the views of his critics:

> When the doctrine [of the Buddha] and the congregation [of monks] are non-existent, how can there be an enlightened one? Speaking in this manner about emptiness, you [i.e., Nagarjuna] contradict the three jewels, as well as the reality of the fruits, both good and bad, and all such worldly convention.[33]

In reply to his critics, Nagarjuna says that they do not understand his use of the word. The critics take emptiness to mean the opposite of real existence. If emptiness annuls being, it must then be the opposite of being: sheer nothingness and chaos and meaninglessness:

> We [Nagarjuna] say that you do not comprehend the purpose of emptiness. As such, you are tormented by emptiness and the meaning of emptiness.
> The teaching of the doctrine by the Buddha is based upon two truths: truth related to worldly convention and truth in terms of ultimate fruit.
> Those who do not understand the distinction between these two truths do not understand the profound truth embodied in the Buddha's message.
> Without relying upon convention, the ultimate fruit is not taught. Without understanding the ultimate fruit, freedom is not attained.[34]

Emptiness is merely a conventional truth, not the ultimate truth. Conventional truths *(lokasamvrtisatya)* have to do with the practical world of making distinctions between good and bad, real and illusory, similarity and difference. For example, conventionally it is useful to know the difference between cabbages and kings, strawberries and deadly nightshade, existence and nonexistence. Ultimate truth *(paramarthata)* is realized in the "right view" of all things as empty. Nagarjuna does not claim that ultimate truth replaces conventional truth. Ultimate truth has no independent existence apart from conventional truths. For example, conventionally speaking, Buddhists say that the Buddha has "entered nirvana." Of course, literally, nirvana is not some "place" that can be "entered." What shall we say of nirvana literally? Nirvana is empty? This too is not true literally, for to take this as a literal truth would be to imply that emptiness exists. What nirvana is literally, the ultimate truth of nirvana, cannot be said literally. The ultimate truth of nirvana can only be communicated through the skillful use of conventional truths about nirvana. This is exactly what Nagarjuna does with his strategy of fourfold negation. Emptiness is merely a word, but a word that is useful for finding release from our attachments. Emptiness is a conventional truth, which, when used strategically, or to use the more traditional Buddhist term, when used *skillfully,* is helpful to Buddhists in their practice of seeking wisdom through non-attachment.

This chapter has focused on the scholarly consensus regarding the Nargarjuna's use of emptiness in the *Stanzas*.[35] Emptiness, as employed skillfully by Nagarjuna, is nothing less than the Buddha's middle path. The Buddha taught a practical religious wisdom that seeks to extinguish the fires of the mind. Nagarjuna is a good Buddhist in this respect. The word *emptiness* is simply a tool useful for Buddhists who seek to detach the mind from its obsessive clinging, to remove fuel from the mind's fire. Used correctly, emptiness is a tool for deconstructing our presuppositions, even our most basic presuppositions about life. For Nagarjuna, however, emptiness is more than an acid for undoing the glue with which we have pieced reality together in our minds. Emptiness is the means by which we are set free from obsessions, including obsessions with speculative theories and religious doctrines. Suffering arises as the mind churns experience into illusions and illusions into attachments to that which is transient, not eternal. Freedom (nirvana) arises when attachments are extinguished. Emptiness has no metaphysical status. Emptiness is merely a word, but a word, we must always hasten to add, that is useful in bringing an end to sorrow. By redirecting our mental energies, we can be set free from sorrow. As the wisdom of the Buddha, emptiness does not become fixated on any metaphysical view of the world. Emptiness is wisdom, but not information about something. Emptiness is not a mental construction or a truth that can be fit snugly into a concept.[36] Mental constructions set the mind on fire. Metaphysical views bind us to *samsara*. Freedom comes by letting go of such obsessions. Because the objects of our desires are empty, we are bound to suffering. But for this same reason, there is the real possibility of the transformation of all our life's energies realizing freedom through non-attachment.

4

Buddhist Emptiness
and the Incomprehensible God

This chapter is an exercise in comparative theology. I would like to ask how Buddhist teachings might become for Christians a resource for their own theological reflections. The exercise at hand will explore a Christian idea, Thomas Aquinas's understanding of what we mean when we say that God is incomprehensible, by comparing it with a Buddhist idea, Nagarjuna's principle of emptiness. This will mean reading Christian texts, a small part of the *Summa Theologiae* and Aquinas's *Commentary on the Gospel of John*, by using a Buddhist text, Nagarjuna's *Stanzas on the Middle Path*. This discussion seeks to disclose the play of similarity and difference that is always at work in the act of skillful comparison. Similarity will lead to insight into difference that in turn will lead to the appreciation of unforeseen similarity and further difference. Unlike the various candidates for a Christian theology of religions, comparative theology is not concerned with showing that Buddhism is, like Christianity, the work of the Holy Spirit. Instead, this exercise is based on the belief that the Buddhist notion of emptiness as developed by Nagarjuna has much to offer Christians as they reflect on the meaning of their own religious tradition.

GOD'S INCOMPREHENSIBILITY IN THOMAS AQUINAS

Despite the many miraculous stories associated with Nagarjuna, we may presume that he probably led the uneventful life of a monk. Even so, his ideas helped to set in motion waves of religious innovation that are still lapping around the shores of Buddhism today. A similar statement can be made of Thomas Aquinas. His was the distinguished but fundamentally undramatic life of a medieval theology professor. Nonetheless, his way of thinking about God has become classic within the Christian tradition.

Aquinas was born in 1225 near Aquino, between Naples and Rome, and entered the Dominicans against the wishes of his family. At the University of Paris, and later in Cologne, Aquinas studied with Albert the Great, a pillar in Scholastic theology and also a Dominican. Having completed his initial studies, Aquinas returned to Paris in 1252 to lecture on the Christian scriptures, a normal step in the process of becoming a full professor in the medieval university system. Then, after almost ten years of teaching in Italian universities, he returned to Paris in 1269 for a second stint there as a professor. In 1272 he went to Italy for teaching duties and died there in 1274.

The doctrine of God's infinite incomprehensibility remains an aspect of Aquinas's theology that richly deserves further discussion.[1] Although pertinent texts can be located in the *Summa Theologiae,* the issue of God's incomprehensibility is most clearly seen in three sequential sections of the *Commentary on the Gospel of John.*[2]

The *Commentary* is based on lectures Aquinas gave during his second stint at the University of Paris. By the time he began this series of lectures, Aquinas had already completed two-thirds of his greatest work, the *Summa Theologiae.* So the *Commentary* and the *Summa* are among his most mature works. The text is not an autograph. During the lectures an assistant to Aquinas took notes that were later corrected by the master. The *Commentary* is a work of medieval Christian theology. In contrast to scriptural commentaries of the patristic period, Aquinas's reflections on the Gospel of John are in the form of classroom lectures, not homilies. In this respect the *Commentary* resembles the *Stanzas.* Both are academic, not homiletic. Nagarjuna's *Stanzas* may reflect his work as a teacher in the Buddhist monastic university of Nalanda. The *Commentary* certainly reflects Aquinas's work as a teacher at the University of Paris. In addition, both works are *theological* in the broad sense of this term. The authors are both monks writing for their co-religionists in a way that reflects the pastoral needs of their readers.

Part One of the *Commentary* deals with the Prologue and first seven chapters of John's Gospel. The eleventh lecture on the first chapter of the Gospel (sections 208–222) is devoted to a discussion of John 1:18:

> No one has ever seen God;
> it is the Only Begotten Son,
> who is in the bosom of the Father,
> who has made him known.

Sections 208–210 address our need for wisdom in the face of human ignorance of God with references to Augustine (no. 209) and the seeming contradictions in other passages of Scripture (no. 210). Then, in section 211, Aquinas asks, "How are we to understand what the evangelist says: 'No one has ever seen God'?"

Section 211 spells out three ways of seeing God. First, God can be seen as a visible form that has been created specifically to represent God. Aquinas calls this visible form a "created substitute" and gives as an example the story in the book of Genesis of God's appearance to Abraham at the oaks of Mamre in the form of three visitors (Gn 18:1–15). Although God does not actually look like the three men who stood before Abraham's tent, the story in Genesis implies that Abraham has had a vision of God. A second way God can be seen is in the form of visions that appear not before the eyes but within the imagination. For example, the prophet Isaiah, standing before the Temple in Jerusalem, has a vision of the Lord God enthroned within the Temple in Jerusalem. In his vision one of the seraphim attending the throne of God takes a burning coal from the altar and purifies the lips of the prophet (Is 6:1–13). In addition to physical forms and presentations to the imagination, there is a third way in which God can be seen. The human mind has the power to move from an experience of the created world to an experience of the One who has created that world. This way of "seeing" God is neither physical nor imaginative but rather intellectual. "[God] is seen by those who, considering the greatness of creatures, see with their intellect the greatness of the Creator." Intellectual visions of God also arise by means of "a certain spiritual light" infused by God during moments of intense contemplation. It is in this latter manner that Jacob can be said to have seen God face to face as during the famous wrestling match in Genesis 32:31.

Then comes a qualification. None of these three forms of seeing God can offer a vision of the essence of God. All three types fail in this regard because nothing visible can capture the fullness of God's essence:

> But the vision of the divine essence is not attained by any of the above visions: for no created species . . . is representative of the divine essence as it is.

Aquinas includes not only physical forms and presentations to the imagination but also intellectual visions. Nothing visible can capture the essence of God because "nothing finite can represent the infinite as it is." Instead of a clear and comprehensive knowledge of the divine essence, physical, imaginative, and intellectual experiences leave us with a knowledge that is "dark and mirrored, and from afar." Thus Aquinas's first point regarding God's incomprehensibility has to do with the inability of something finite to grasp, encompass, plumb, or comprehend the infinite. The incomprehensibility of the divine results from the utter lack of proportion that exists between the infinite God and the finite mind of the human being, or what Aquinas calls the created intellect.

In regard to the question of our experience of God, Aquinas remains a consistent empiricist. All our knowledge, including our knowledge of God, has its ultimate beginnings in a concrete experience of the world. Based on sense experience human beings begin to inquire into the ultimate principles that govern the nature and behavior of things. These metaphysical questions, in due course, lead to a natural curiosity about God. Only after being concerned with material things is the mind eventually led to a knowledge of God. Aquinas's empiricism allows him to make two important points. First, even though God does not appear within the world as an object, all human beings have an implicit knowledge of God simply by being involved in the material world.[3] Second, since it is rooted in a concrete experience of the world, every act of knowing is limited to some degree. In section 211 of the *Commentary*, Aquinas speaks of knowledge in the form of a "created species," by which he means some finite image or concept or notion that forms a part of our experience of the created world. In order to think of God as being everywhere and eternal, we must rely on our concrete experience of space and time. In thinking of God as omnipotent, the religious imagination brings into play concrete experiences of power at work in the world. Yet no matter how resourceful our religious imagination might be, nothing in our experience can fully represent God:

> Therefore, the knowledge by which God is seen through creatures is not a knowledge of his essence, but a knowledge that is dark and mirrored, and from afar.

Thus God remains incomprehensibly beyond the reach of all our images and concepts. The finite cannot contain within itself the infinite without imposing some limitation on the infinite. God is incomprehensible to the human mind because of the radical disproportion between the finite intellect and the infinity of the divine.

Are we to conclude, then, that no human being will ever behold the essence of God? Since the human mind is finite and the imagination relies on concrete images and concepts, one might expect such a conclusion from Aquinas. Section 212, however, argues against such a view using a doctrinal argument. Those who claim that human beings will never behold the divine essence have taken a position that is contrary to Christian faith. To believe this is "false and heretical" for three reasons. First, citing 1 John 3:2 and John 17:3, this view is seen to be contrary to the teachings of scripture. The second argument has to do with implicit knowledge. God is not seen by human beings in the same way an object within the world is seen. Things within the world are visible because they reflect light that shines on them from without. God, however, is unique. God is the light by which we see light itself. For Aquinas, this means that, in our ordinary experience of the world ("seeing light"), we have an implicit knowledge of the "light by which we see light," which is the essence of God. Third, Aquinas reminds the reader that, in accordance with Christian teaching, "it is impossible for anyone to attain perfect happiness except in the vision of the divine essence." For all creatures, happiness consists in the fulfillment of their specific natures. In the case of human beings, human nature finds fulfillment in knowing, which in its fullest form becomes love. Happiness for human beings, therefore, consists of fulfilling human nature by knowing and loving. Naturally, human beings desire to know the foundation of all things, which is God. To be denied this knowledge would imply that human beings can never be completely happy:

> Therefore, to take away the possibility of the vision of the divine essence by man is to take away happiness itself. Therefore, in order for the created intellect to be happy, it is necessary that the divine essence be seen.

Therefore, Christian faith in the ultimate happiness of human beings requires us to affirm that God's essence can be known. Aquinas quotes scripture in support of this view: "Blessed are the pure of heart, for they shall see God" (Mt 5:8). Although God remains incomprehensible to human beings due to the disproportion between God's infinite essence and the finite limits of the mind, here Aquinas wants to remind the reader that the promise of a full vision of God can be expected with the assurance of faith.

In sections 211 and 212 of the *Commentary* Aquinas has been setting up a problem. On the one hand, God is incomprehensible because the finite cannot comprehend the infinite. On the other hand, human beings can be ultimately happy only by being fulfilled by a knowledge of God's essence. Furthermore, Christians must believe that they will achieve ultimate happiness as a tenant of their faith. How can all this be true? Section 213 is intriguing because Aquinas does not resolve the contradiction between Christian faith and metaphysical necessity, as one might expect.

In section 213 Aquinas once again makes three points. First, in keeping with the disproportion between the infinite and the finite established in section 211, the divine essence will never be seen by the eye, which can only see "sensate bodily things." Second, we are told that

> as long as the human intellect is in the body it cannot see God, because it is weighed down by the body so that it cannot attain the summit of contemplation.

Reasoning such as this would seem to have a clear aim. One might expect Aquinas to argue that once the intellect is freed from the body by death and has entered into the fullness of the contemplation of God in the beatific vision in heaven, then human beings will be able to see the divine essence as Christian faith teaches. Aquinas's third point, however, comes as a surprise:

> No created intellect (however abstracted, either by death, or separated from the body) which does see the divine essence, can comprehend it in any way.

One might expect Aquinas to solve the problem by claiming that death separates us from our finite bodies, and thus from the disproportion of the infinite God and the finite mind. Once we are freed from our finite bodies, the disproportion of the infinite God and the finite intellect no longer exists and God is no longer incomprehensible. However, Aquinas refuses to take this route. Even in the beatific vision, that is, after the death of the body and the entry of the soul into heaven, God remains incomprehensible.

Thus, the *Commentary* presents us with a considerable problem for understanding. In order to reach an adequate grasp of Aquinas's teaching regarding the incomprehensibility of God, three separate claims must be reconciled. First, Aquinas claims that God's incomprehensibility results from a disproportion between the infinity of God and the finitude of the human mind. This claim is made in section 211. Second, Aquinas claims that God remains incomprehensible even in the beatific vision. This claim is the surprise that comes in section 213. And yet despite this state of affairs, Aquinas's own Christian faith requires him to claim that the ultimate happiness of the human person, which can be fulfilled only in the complete vision of God's essence, is a revealed doctrine of faith. This claim is clearly stated in section 212. An adequate interpretation of Aquinas requires that points one and two somehow be understood so as not to exclude point three. In other words, Aquinas's doctrine of the incomprehensibility of God demands that we understand the immediate vision of God in the beatific vision in such a way that God's incomprehensibility is preserved, not overcome. In addition, we must understand the incomprehensibility of God in a way that does not diminish the fullness of the beatific vision.

THE INFINITELY KNOWABLE GOD

In the twenty-second chapter of the *Stanzas*, in the midst of his discussion of the emptiness of the Tathagata, Nagarjuna cautions against objectifying emptiness into some kind of metaphysical absolute:

> "Empty," "non-empty," "both" or "neither"—these should not be declared.
> It is expressed only for the purpose of communication.[4]

What is it that Nagarjuna wishes to communicate? Nagarjuna was a monk writing for monks. The only purpose Nagarjuna has in using a noun—in fact, an abstract noun—like *emptiness (sunyata)* would be to communicate something useful to his monastic students. Used properly, emptiness is a tool for prying loose attachments to ideas generated by a feverish mind. The objects of our obsessions, even when our obsessions are great Buddhist doctrines like nirvana and the Tathagata, are constructions of the mind. They arise by means of dependent origination and are completely empty of inherent self-existence *(svabhava)*. In using a term like *emptiness,* what Nagarjuna wants to communicate is not another theory about the ultimate nature of reality. Rather, Nagarjuna wants to impress upon his students the Buddhist wisdom of freedom through non-attachment.

Like Nagarjuna, Aquinas is also a monk writing for monks and has a religious truth to communicate. Nagarjuna's exposition of the principle of emptiness is completely in the service of promoting the Buddhist diagnosis of our human predicament—attachment to false views. In this respect Nagarjuna is useful in trying to understand what Aquinas is up to in the *Commentary*. In section 213 of the *Commentary*, Aquinas asks why God remains incomprehensible to the intellect in the beatific vision even after death. Before giving his own answer to this question, Aquinas examines and then rejects an explanation that would seem appropriate, at least at first. One might explain the persistence of God's incomprehensibility in the beatific vision by concluding that the soul cannot enjoy a complete vision of God's essence in heaven. Because of this lack of knowledge, God remains incomprehensible:

> And so it is commonly said that although the whole divine essence is seen by the blessed, since it is most simple and has no parts, yet it is not wholly seen, because this would be to comprehend it. . . . Hence one who does not see him wholly does not comprehend him.

Christian faith, however, does not allow Aquinas to believe that some part of God remains forever concealed to human beings, whose final happiness lies only in knowing God fully and completely. Instead, God remains incomprehensible in the beatific vision not because a part of God remains forever *unknowable*, but rather because God is *infinitely knowable:*

> And since God is infinite in power and being, and as a consequence is infinitely knowable, he cannot be known by any created intellect to the degree that he is knowable. And thus he remains incomprehensible to every created intellect.

God is incomprehensible, even in the beatific vision, not because a part of God remains concealed to the intellect and only partially knowable. God's incomprehensibility is rooted in the fact that God can be known again and again, in ever more profound ways. In support of this view Aquinas cites the book of Job: "Behold, God is great, exceeding our knowledge" (Jb 36:26). Instead of the language of concealment and privation, we are given the image of a God whose ability to be known always exceeds the capacity of the mind to comprehend.

As noted earlier, the *Commentary* was based on lectures on the Gospel of John given in 1269, after the majority of his most famous work, the *Summa Theologiae*, had been written. In Part One, question twelve of the *Summa*, Aquinas makes a statement rather similar to his observation in the *Commentary* about God being infinitely knowable. This part of the *Summa* illuminates what Aquinas is doing in the *Commentary*. The twelfth question has to do with how God is known by his creatures. In the seventh article, Aquinas asks, "Can a created mind comprehend the essence of God?" In the "reply" section, we are given a negative answer to this question. To comprehend means to understand a thing perfectly; to understand perfectly is to understand a thing as well as it can be understood. Therefore God is incomprehensible, even in the beatific vision, because no finite act of understanding can exhaust the infinite depths of God:

> Now no created mind can attain the perfect sort of understanding that is intrinsically possible of God's essence. This is made evident as follows: each thing can be understood to the extent that it is actually realized. God therefore, whose actual being is infinite . . . can be infinitely understood.[5]

In the *Commentary* Aquinas speaks of God as infinitely knowable. In the *Summa* God is infinitely understandable. Both the *Commentary* and the *Summa* are noteworthy for what Aquinas does not say. Aquinas never claims that God's incomprehensibility results from the fact that there is a part of God that remains eternally denied to the finite intellect in the human quest for fulfillment through knowledge. Instead, we read the following in the *Summa:*

> When we say that God is not comprehended we do not mean there is something about him that is not seen, but that he cannot be seen as perfectly as intrinsically he is visible.[6]

In the beatific vision God's persistent incomprehensibility results not from a deficit in the shining light of God's glory (the *lumen gloriae*) or a decision on God's part to remain unrevealed. On the contrary, the beatific vision is a vision of God fully revealed. In fact, it would seem that God is fully incomprehensible only when fully revealed in the beatific vision.

In rooting God's incomprehensibility in God's unlimited ability to be known, Aquinas succeeds in avoiding two alternatives unacceptable to him as a Christian believer. On the one hand, if God's incomprehensibility resulted merely from the disproportion between the infinity of God and the finite mind, as discussed in section 211, then the final happiness of the human person could never be attained, a violation of Christian faith according to section 212. The human being's natural desire for fulfillment through knowing the truth would be infinitely enkindled by the experience of knowing the world and infinitely frustrated by the experience of some aspect of God eternally concealed to the mind and its quest for knowledge. In the "Inferno" section of Dante's *Divine Comedy*, a poem that even modest examination reveals to have been greatly influenced by the theology of Thomas Aquinas, the "virtuous pagans," those who have died without sin but also without the benefit of baptism, are consigned to limbo, a purely natural paradise illuminated by the light of reason, not the *lumen gloriae* of heaven. Despite all its natural pleasures, Dante places limbo within the front gate of hell, for limbo is indeed a place of punishment. Virgil, Dante's guide through hell and a resident of limbo, explains this punishment to Dante with a chilling comment, "Without hope, we live on in desire."[7] The desire of which Virgil speaks is the desire for God. All human beings have a natural desire to fulfill their human nature by knowing the truth. This natural desire can ultimately be fulfilled only in a knowledge of God.

On the other hand, if God were ultimately comprehensible in the beatific vision, contrary to the position Aquinas takes in section 213, then by completely comprehending God the human mind would in effect transcend God. In this case the ultimate happiness of the human person could never be attained (once again, a violation of Christian faith). God would become but another object within human consciousness that can be discarded after it is no longer fulfilling or interesting. Frederick Nietzsche would have the last laugh: by fully comprehending God, human beings would witness the death of God as a transcendent force in human life. In this death of God every human being would be burdened with the unhappy obligation of being his or her own god.

Thus Aquinas's position is that God's incomprehensibility is not a matter of concealment but of disclosure. Here, a comparison with Nagarjuna is useful for understanding Aquinas more deeply. Nagarjuna uses the principle of emptiness as a way to pry loose our attachments to our false views of nirvana, the Tathagata, and even of emptiness itself. Implied in Aquinas's doctrine of divine incomprehensibility is his own Christian concern for "views." If God remains incomprehensible even in the beatific vision because God is infinitely knowable, then every concrete image or concept the mind forms of God is rendered inadequate by the fact that further knowledge of the infinitely knowable God is always being revealed. Thus, any attempt to objectify once and for all our understanding of

God into a static image or rigid concept will be undercut by the endless ability of God to be known anew. Nagarjuna speaks, in Buddhist fashion, of "false views." Aquinas, of course, does not use this Buddhist language. Our views of God are not false in the Buddhist sense. Rather, they are inadequate and preliminary, no matter how profound.

Even in this initial comparison of Nagarjuna and Aquinas, the play of similarity and difference can be seen. Both of these religious thinkers are interested in views as part of religious quests, one Buddhist and the other Christian. For Nagarjuna, the views are always false views that must be renounced in the Buddhist quest for freedom through non-attachment. For Aquinas, the views in question are not necessarily false, but they are always preliminary. Not all views of God are false, at least in the Buddhist sense of false views. All views, however, are inadequate, even views of God that are true.

TWO VISIONS OF THE RELIGIOUS QUEST

Emptiness and incomprehensibility, each in its own way, render a service to Buddhists and Christians. They help to clarify Buddhist and Christian affirmations about what it means to be fully human. Both Christianity and Buddhism hold up to the world ideals of what a worthwhile human life should be. Emptiness, for Nagarjuna, and incomprehensibility, for Aquinas, are conceptual tools for clarifying what a worthwhile life is for their respective faiths. In enunciating his notion of emptiness as the wisdom of non-attachment, Nagarjuna never loses track of his fundamentally religious concerns as a Buddhist monk by straying into purely speculative philosophy. Emptiness must always be understood in tandem with the universal problem of human suffering and the Buddhist quest to realize freedom (nirvana) from suffering. Nagarjuna's exclusively religious concern suggests a model for appreciating Aquinas's doctrine of divine incomprehensibility. What Aquinas has to say about God's incomprehensibility must never be separated from Christianity's understanding of the ultimate happiness of the human person in a full knowledge of God.

Thus both emptiness and incomprehensibility are intimately connected with Buddhist and Christian claims about human life and its capacity for fulfillment through some sort of religious transformation. The Buddhist tradition is rich in terminology for speaking about this transformation. In early Buddhist literature, a term like "nirvana," which has been translated into English with terms as diverse as "annihilation," "extinction," "liberation" and "freedom," is complimented by terms such as "enlightenment" *(bodhi)* and "deliverance" *(moksa).* For present purposes, let the term "awakening" serve as a generic term for the Buddhist understanding of transformation. Christianity also has a vocabulary rich in terms for speaking about religious transformation, none of which is exactly equivalent. Christian tradition speaks of salvation, redemption, and in more recent times, conversion. A term featured prominently in Aquinas's discussion of God's incomprehensibility in the *Commentary* is *beatitudo*, which can be translated as "beatitude" or "happiness." For Aquinas and the Christian tradition more generally, beatitude refers to the happiness of human beings that arises in the fulfillment of their nature through a knowledge of God. Nagarjuna cannot properly conceive of Buddhist awakening without emptiness. Likewise, Aquinas cannot conceive of a human being's final beatitude without God being incomprehensible.

In effect, both emptiness and incomprehensibility are strategies for making a positive affirmation about the human person. Human beings, ultimately, are not bound by either false views, in the Buddhist sense, or by an ignorance of God, in the Christian sense. For all their differences, both of these concepts are part of positive religious visions of what it means to be fulfilled as a human being. As a Buddhist, Nagarjuna looks on the world and all that is found in it as utterly transient *(anicca)*. Suffering *(dukkha)* arises when the mind churns its illusions into attachments that reify life into static concepts. Suffering ceases when attachments cease. Emptiness is a useful tool for Buddhists grappling with false views. Affirming the emptiness of all views, in effect, is a Buddhist way of affirming that human fulfillment is possible. For Aquinas, the fulfillment of the human person consists in a beatifying knowledge of God. This beatitude can be hoped for with the assurance of Christian faith. As noted above, the human person's ultimate happiness would be impossible if a part of God remained eternally concealed to the created intellect. Like the denizens of Dante's limbo, human beings would live with the eternally unfulfilled desire to know what God refuses to reveal. Likewise, the human person's ultimate happiness would be impossible if God were ultimately understandable. As in Nietzsche's vision of the death of God, the human person would understand all of God and then step out into the void beyond God hungry for more knowledge. The final fulfillment of the human person, an unending intimacy with God, is possible only if God's incomprehensibility is a function of God's infinite ability to be known. Like emptiness, God's incomprehensibility is a way to affirm that human fulfillment is possible.

Each in its own way, emptiness and incomprehensibility offer a positive assessment of the human situation: the human person is not bound. In Nagarjuna's case we are not bound to attachments, even attachments to nirvana and the Tathagata. In Aquinas's case we are not bound by any understanding of God, even an orthodox understanding. Both notions are integral parts of differing religious views of human fulfillment. If Aquinas is to succeed in affirming the human person's unlimited potential for beatitude, he must locate the incomprehensibility of God in God's infinite capacity to be known. If Nagarjuna is to succeed in affirming the human person's unlimited potential for freedom from attachments, he must also argue for the emptiness not only of nirvana and the Tathagata but also he must show that emptiness itself is empty. If God is not incomprehensible in the Christian context and if emptiness is not empty in the Buddhist, then the human person is ultimately bound and not fulfilled.[8]

TRANSFORMATION WITHOUT TRANSCENDENCE

The city of Chartres in northern France is justly famous for its Gothic cathedral. Architectural lines in this building soar heavenward for hundreds of feet before converging in a way that the stones appear to float. The soul wants to follow the architectural lines in their ascent into heaven. In fact, the cathedral itself might rightly be thought of as a metaphor for the soul's journey into God. Like Chartres, the city of Kyoto in Japan is also renowned for its religiously inspired architecture. In the northwest corner of the city lies the Temple of the Dragon's Rest, Ryoan-ji, with its famous rock garden.[9] Here, in contrast to Chartres, the architectural lines are very close to the ground. The arrangement of stairways and thresholds, verandahs and walls, gardens and passageways are designed to dissolve the distinction between the natural world and the humanly constructed world. At Ryoan-ji the soul is not invited to ascend into the heavens. The rocks, the medieval walls with their tiles and patina, the play of earth tones and pure white, the confusion of inside and outside—all these elements combine to draw one's attention to the things of this world. Only, now, the world is strangely silent and wondrous to behold because it is unencumbered by the need to symbolize anything beyond itself. The *Stanzas* were first brought to Japan with the introduction of Buddhist thought in the seventh century. Since that time the notion of emptiness has asserted a considerable influence on the development of Japan's culture. As the cathedral in Chartres was inspired by the Christian notion of God's transcendence, Ryoan-ji in Kyoto realizes in wood and stone Buddhist emptiness.

The obvious architectural differences that distinguish Chartres from Ryoan-ji serve as a warning against being overly eager to equate Aquinas's incomprehensible God and Nagarjuna's emptiness. Aquinas's God is not incomprehensible in the way that Nagarjuna's emptiness is empty. As noted in the discussion of the fulfillment model of religious diversity, underscoring similarities while marginalizing differences runs the considerable risk of sheltering Christianity from the need to test its self-understanding against the otherness of religious paths outside itself. The sizable differences separating Aquinas and Nagarjuna may prove to be greater resources for Christian theological reflection than even the significant similarities.

One significant similarity linking Nagarjuna's emptiness with Aquinas's incomprehensibility has been found in the function each principle performs within Buddhist and Christian notions of human fulfillment. Both emptiness and incomprehensibility are, in effect, positive statements about human beings and their capacity for finding fulfillment through some kind of religious transformation. Both are concepts deeply embedded within complex religious narratives about what it means to be human. If Aquinas is to affirm, as his Christian faith requires him to affirm, a human being's unlimited capacity for beatitude, he must locate God's incomprehensibility to the finite intellect in God's ability to be known infinitely. If Nagarjuna is to affirm, as his Buddhist beliefs requires of him, a human being's infinite capacity for awakening, he must recognize the emptiness not only of nirvana and the Tathagata, but even the emptiness of emptiness itself. Buddhists and Christians, however, imagine human fulfillment in rather different ways. Where Christians speak in terms of unending beatitude and unlimited transcendence into God, Buddhists speak of awakening, not to a God beyond this world, but to freedom from suffering.

The awakening envisioned in the *Stanzas* entails a radical transformation of life without presupposing an experience of transcendence beyond this world. Herein lies a difference distinguishing Nagarjuna from Aquinas that is lasting, significant, and that opens up a line of inquiry whose potential for insight will not soon be exhausted by Buddhists and Christians in conversation with one another. Nagarjuna uses his fourfold logic of negation to exclude the possibility of understanding nirvana as a transcendent realm beyond this world. The realization of release from attachments does not lead beyond this world into a transcendent realm. The historical Buddha, at least as he was depicted in early Buddhist literature, spoke of human existence as fettered to the realm of illusion *(samsara).* However, unlike other religious teachers in the India of his day, the Buddha remained silent about the existence of a metaphysical ultimate out of which the world of illusion arises (Brahman). This silence also applies to the existence of a transcendental realm of ideal truths, as Plato taught. The historical Buddha did speak about heavenly realms. In fact, he spoke of multiple heavens crowded with gods. But quite clearly these heavens, in the preaching of the Buddha, are included within the realm of *samsara.* Even the gods are dependently arisen and subject to karmic law; they are not the God known to Christianity. In this sense Nagarjuna's use of the principle of emptiness to construct a Buddhist model of the transformation of life systematically deconstructs the idea of a transcendent God that lies at the heart of Aquinas's doctrine of incomprehensibility and even Aquinas's understanding of human fulfillment.

Transcendence, unfortunately, is a term bursting at the seams with ambiguities and associations that have been heaped onto it over the centuries. I use the term in the more technical sense that Christianity has inherited from Plato's philosophy and more directly from the neo-Platonism of Plotinus. The *transcendent* refers to a metaphysical unity beyond the changing world of the senses.[10] The term can be applied to Buddhist awakening only in a more generic sense. To become awakened or enlightened is to experience a kind of transcendence, but not the Platonic transcendence presumed by Aquinas. In the *Stanzas* emptiness functions as a tool for bringing about a reorientation of subjectivity. In the awakening through non-attachment envisioned by Buddhism, the direction of life, along with the values and commitments that shape life, undergoes a transformation. Calling this transformation transcendence, however, runs the risk of confusing the subtlety of Ryoan-ji for the majesty of Chartres.

VIA NEGATIVA?

The absence of transcendence, at least in the sense familiar to Aquinas, signals another difference between the *Stanzas* and the *Commentary* that might otherwise go unnoticed. The principle of negation at work at the heart of Nagarjuna's notion of emptiness does not lead to the *via negativa* (way of negation) for which Aquinas is so famous.

Aquinas is no stranger to the strategic use of negation for a religious end. Following Aristotle, Aquinas believed that our knowledge begins with an experience of the world. The mind is first concerned with material things before its natural desire for fulfillment through knowledge leads it to ask metaphysical questions. These metaphysical questions, in turn, direct the person's quest for fulfillment to a knowledge of God. A real knowledge of God, however, does not imply, for Aquinas, that human beings escape the limitations of the mind, which is ensconced in this world of concrete experience. All knowledge is rooted in images or concepts (what Aquinas calls "phantasms") derived in one way or another from sense experience. On this topic we find the following passage in the *Summa:*

> For the mind actually to understand something there is required an act of the imagination . . . not only in receiving fresh knowledge but also in using knowledge already acquired. . . . Anyone can experience for himself that when he tries to understand something he forms for himself some images by way of example in which he can see, as it were, what he is trying to understand. Hence also when we wish to make anyone understand something we set before him examples from which he can form for himself images with a view to understanding.[11]

This rule applies even to our knowledge of God. In every encounter with the divine, God is imagined in some way or another. For example, in thinking of God as present everywhere, the mind at least implicitly is understanding God using its experience of space. In imagining God to be eternal, the mind is using its experience of time.[12] The fact that knowledge has its beginnings in a concrete experience of material things suggests that all our knowledge of God is inadequate or, as Aquinas states in section 211 of the *Commentary*, "dark and mirrored, and from afar."

The material beginnings of knowledge also suggests that we arrive at a knowledge of God by means of an ascent beyond the world of appearances. Moving from our experiences of this world to a vision of God is an act of transcendence accomplished by a method of negation:

> Because we cannot know what God is, but rather what God is not, our method has to be mainly negative.
> What kind of being God is not can be known by eliminating characteristics which cannot apply to Him, like composition, change, and so forth.[13]

By successively denying the appropriateness of certain finite characteristics as descriptions of the divine essence, God is seen more and more truly. God is not this, God is not that. In this fashion God comes to be known more profoundly in terms of what God is not than by any attempt at naming directly the divine essence.[14]

But in a way that is vastly different from Nagarjuna's use of negation, Aquinas holds that there are some concepts that apply to God directly and are not to be negated. For example, God is wise and good. Statements such as this are not to be negated in reaching for a yet more profound understanding of the divine. In contrast to Aquinas, Nagarjuna applies his own strategy of negation even to the most basic of Buddhist doctrines. Aquinas employs negation more sparingly. The difference between these strategies of negation sheds light on the differences that distinguish Nagarjuna's emptiness from Aquinas's incomprehensibility and Buddhist awakening from Christian beatitude.[15]

More specifically, Nagarjuna's fourfold negation does not lead to an ascent of the soul into God. The fourth line of Nagarjuna's fourfold negation (neither/nor) is also rejected by Nagarjuna as a possible view of either the Tathagata or nirvana. This neither/nor bears a decided resemblance to what Christian theology knows as the *via negativa*. Nagarjuna was well aware of this strategy from his familiarity with Hindu philosophers of his own day who were working within the tradition of the Upanishads. In the Upanishads and the commentarial tradition that flows from them, Ultimate Reality (Brahman) is known by means of a "not this, not that" *(neti-neti)*. If Nagarjuna has the Upanishads in mind when he argues against taking a neither/nor approach, the injunction against neither/nor would seem to apply to Aquinas's *via negativa* as well. A right view of nirvana is not gained by claiming nirvana is successively "neither this nor that, neither this nor that." This would imply that nirvana is a transcendent realm that has inherent self-existence *(svabhava)* that can be known progressively by means of successive negations of preliminary views. For Aquinas, in contrast, the *via negativa* constitutes a suitable strategy to employ in our quest for an ever deeper knowledge of the infinitely knowable God. Nagarjuna's use of negation is not in the service of a mystical ascent into a transcendent God. It is not about an ascent into nirvana understood as a transcendent realm beyond *samsara*. Awakening is not even about a "journey" into the "emptiness of all." Instead of something that transcends this world, emptiness is no different from the process of dependent arising itself.[16] Instead of a journey that takes the soul from the created to the Uncreated, Buddhist awakening leads us to a greater intimacy and more compassionate relationship with what is perfectly ordinary.

EMPTINESS AS THE NEGATION OF HOLINESS

In section 211 of the *Commentary*, Aquinas makes reference to the vision of the Prophet Isaiah enthroned within the Holy of Holies of the Temple in Jerusalem:

> In the year of King Uzziah's death I saw the Lord seated on a throne, high and exalted, and the skirt of his robe filled the temple. About him were attendant seraphim, and each had six wings; one pair covered his face and one pair his feet, and one pair was spread in flight. They were calling ceaselessly to one another,
> > Holy, holy, holy is the Lord of Hosts:
> > the whole earth is full of his glory. (Is 6:1–3)

Isaiah's vision has become for Christians a classic image of God as Cosmic Monarch. As the seraphim proclaim the holiness of the Lord God, the Temple is shaken to its foundations. Isaiah responds to the vision with fear,

Woe is me! I am lost
For I am a man of unclean lips
and I dwell among a people of unclean lips;
yet with these eyes I have seen the King, the Lord of
    Hosts. (Is 6:5)

The holiness of God is here measured by the majesty of God towering above the lowliness of the prophet, the glory of the divine shining down on the world and its pollution. In revealing himself to Isaiah, God has also revealed the great distance that separates the sacred from the profane. In coming to stand in awe before this distance separating heaven and earth, human beings also come to know God as the Holy One.

A stark contrast can be drawn between the image of God evoked by Isaiah and the following story attributed to Tan-hsia T'ien-jan (738–824), a Buddhist monk of the T'ang Dynasty in China. Tan-hsia was a monk of the Zen tradition in China. He would have looked upon Nagarjuna as a patriarch of his lineage. After stopping at a well-established temple in the Chinese capital for a night, he was shown into the main hall dominated by a triptych of statues. The weather was so severely cold that he took one of the statues from the main hall and made a fire with it in order to warm himself. The monk charged with maintaining the hall, on seeing Tan-hsia's fire, became greatly agitated. "How dare you burn my wooden Buddha!" Tan-hsia stirred the ashes with a stick and replied, "I am gathering the holy *sariras*." A *sarira* is an indestructible substance, generally in pebble form, found in the body of a saint when cremated. Growing increasingly agitated, the monk asked, "How can you get *sariras* by burning a wooden Buddha?" Tan-hsia's reply was quick: "If there are no *sariras* to be found in it, may I have the remaining two Buddhas for my fire?"[17]

Isaiah knows as well as Tan-hsia that statues are but human constructions of wood. No statue should be equated with the "holy God of power and might." Only God is holy, not any statue of God. This is not Tan-hsia's point, however. In burning the statue of the Buddha, Tan-hsia rejects not only attachment to precious statues but attachment to the Buddha as well. In this respect he showed himself to be a good student of Nagarjuna. To look on the Tathagata as a transcendent God is a false view and not helpful for finding freedom from suffering. As there are no *sariras* to be found in the statue of the Buddha, neither are there *sariras* to be found in the Tathagata. When the Chinese Zen master Lin Chi says, "When meeting a Buddha, slay the Buddha; When meeting a Patriarch, slay the Patriarch,"[18] he is offering the same insight in the form of an aphorism that Nagarjuna captures in a more logical form, that is, do not say the Buddha exists, does not exist, both/and, neither/nor.

The modern world has called into question Christianity's traditional understanding of God as the transcendent Holy One. Isaiah's vision of God as Lord of Hosts, so plausible to Aquinas and his contemporaries, is decidedly less credible today. With the coming of the Copernican revolution and especially after the rise of the Newtonian "world system," there was no longer much need for a divine Monarch to rule over the universe and keep the planets in their courses.

Increasingly, the world could be seen as self-explanatory.[19] This modern development led to revisionist accounts of God's holiness. In the philosophy of Immanuel Kant (1724–1804), for example, the holiness of God is not a matter of his transcendent majesty. Holiness is a moral quality. God is holy not by being the Lord of Hosts and Ruler over the universe, but as a postulate of moral reason. In 1917 Rudolf Otto began a reaction against Kant with the publication of *The Idea of the Holy*.[20] Otto acknowledged the moral quality of holiness but also saw the need to recognize that holiness goes beyond morality to include elements of raw power. As in Isaiah's vision, holiness is disclosed to human beings as a *mysterium tremendum et facinans*, a mystery that evokes both fear and wonderment. Neo-Orthodox theologians in the mid-twentieth century went beyond Otto in emphasizing the gulf between Creator and creature. For Karl Barth, for instance, holiness is a matter of God's utter transcendence. In fact, God is the "completely other" *(ganz Anderer)*.[21] Emile Brunner thinks of God's holiness in terms of the chasm separating the divine from the mundane.

Shin'ichi Hisamatsu, a Japanese Buddhist rooted in the Zen lineage, taught for many years in Kyoto. Hisamatsu argued that if the Christian God is holy by being transcendent, Buddhist emptiness must be seen as the negation of God's holiness.[22] If the holiness of God is disclosed in the confrontation with the awesome distance that separates the divine from the mundane, then the principle of emptiness deconstructs that distance. Thus, instead of the metaphors of depth and distance that have become so basic to the way Christians speak about God, Buddhism prefers what Bernard Faure has called the "rhetoric of immediacy."[23] Terms familiar to Christians, like "*trans*-cendence" into the "*super*-natural," reflect Christianity's early encounter with Greek thought. Terms such as these imply that there is a "higher" reality "beyond" the appearances of this world, in keeping with Plato's understanding of reality. Instead of metaphors of depth and distance, Japanese Buddhists speak of the "suchness" (Japanese = *shin-nyo*; Sanskrit = *tathata*) of things and use phrases like "the original naturalness of all" *(jinen-honi)* that arises after we renounce our false views.[24] Take for example this statement from another famous Chinese monk of the T'ang dynasty, Zen Master Ch'ing-yüan Wei-hsin:

> Thirty years ago, before I began the study of Zen, I said, "Mountains are mountains and waters are waters." After I got an insight into the truth of Zen through the instruction of a good master, I said, "Mountains are not mountains, waters are not waters." But now, having attained the abode of final rest [awakening], I say, "Mountains are really mountains, waters are really waters."[25]

In the conventional world of false views, mountains are mountains and rivers are rivers. Zen practice begins to erode our attachments to false views and the distortion of reality that an egocentric perspective brings with it. In this process of deconstructing false views, mountains are no longer mountains, waters are no longer waters. Finally, after awakening, Ch'ing-yüan can see that mountains are really nothing other than mountains. They are not a challenge to the ego to be conquered by climbing. They are not pieces of real estate to be purchased. They are really mountains and nothing else. More important, Ch'ing-yüan does not look on mountains as symbols of a transcendent reality that lies beyond them. They are not, as in Christian tradition, raw material for an analogy of being that would lead his soul on a journey into God—what Aquinas's colleague at the University of Paris, Bonaventure, called an *itinerarium mentis in deum*. Like the story of Isaiah's vision of God enthroned in the Jerusalem Temple, Ch'ing-yüan's lines present us with a narrative about a religious vision. But unlike the passage from Isaiah, the Buddhist account does not contain any reference to a transcendent divinity. Ch'ing-yüan Wei-hsin's awakening does not lead to transcendence into holiness. Instead, Ch'ing-yüan is led to a right view of this world and the ordinary things that populate it. Mountains are really nothing more than mountains. Waters are really nothing more than waters. This is what Buddhism means when it uses terms like *suchness* and *the original naturalness of all.*

Herein lies a real difference separating Nagarjuna from Aquinas and Buddhists from Christians. In comparative theology, some Christians should expect to find both similarities and differences when they begin to think about their own religious tradition by comparing it with another. In this case the careful reading of the *Stanzas* and the *Commentary* does not suggest that Buddhism and Christianity are but variations on a common religious essence. Emptiness and incomprehensibility are not two different names for a reality that transcends all religions, contrary to what many pluralist philosophers would argue. Is emptiness an indication that the Holy Spirit, witnessed to by Christian faith, is at work in Nagarjuna and his followers down to this day? Certainly Christians may say this without contradicting their own faith in the Holy Spirit. Taking such a position, however, does nothing to help Christians in understanding and appreciating Buddhists better. In fact, this fulfillment theology does much to obscure what Nagarjuna is trying to say. Shin'ichi Hisamatsu has noted that suchness is the negation of the holiness of the Christian God. In dialogue, I have noted that the Christian God is the negation of Buddhist suchness. Christianity is witness to the God who eternally remains creation's "other." To equate the God of Abraham, Isaac, and Jacob with the suchness of Buddhism or with Nagarjuna's emptiness does violence to both Christianity and Buddhism. The otherness of Christianity's God cannot be incorporated into the totality of the world realized as suchness.

EMPTINESS AND GRACE

Nagarjuna is a logician. In the *Stanzas* he develops the principle of emptiness as a logical tool of analysis for breaking down the false views that breed attachment. Aquinas, in contrast, is a theologian. In saying this, I do not mean to imply that Aquinas is philosophically unsophisticated. In fact, the contrary is the case. Aquinas is a theologian in the sense that, in developing his doctrine of divine incomprehensibility, he is responding to not only the demands of reason but also the revealed truths of Christian faith. He looks upon God's incomprehensibility as a revealed truth, not merely a logically coherent concept demanded by the disproportion of the infinite God to a finite intellect. Aquinas holds that God becomes fully incomprehensible only when God is fully revealed in an act of self-disclosure to a finite intellect. Divine incomprehensibility, therefore, is a part of Aquinas's theological witness to the saving initiatives of the living God, as this God chooses to reveal. God's true incomprehensibility can be known only to the extent that God reveals, not by human reason alone. Therefore, the incomprehensibility of God is a truth that "happens" to a human being as an "event" within the spiritual life.

There is a time-honored story about Aquinas that illustrates this very point. Toward the end of his life, while he was still finishing the *Summa Theologiae*, Aquinas was given a mystical vision of God while he was saying mass. According to tradition, after this event Aquinas put down his quill and never wrote another word. In fact, he is reputed to have dismissed his great theological writings as mere "straw." Aquinas himself, however, would want to draw attention to ordinary acts of faith, hope, and love as moments in which the human person is transformed by transcendence into the incomprehensible God. The realization of divine incomprehensibility through the event of God's self-disclosure may be dramatically set off from ordinary life, as in the anecdote about Aquinas, or seamlessly circumscribed by it. In either case a human person realizes the incomprehensibility of God not by reason alone but by means of the revelatory event of God's active self-disclosure.

Nagarjuna is not a theist like Aquinas. His doctrine of emptiness is not part of a theological witness to the saving action of a transcendent God. If incomprehensibility is a form of Christian witness to divine initiative, then emptiness should be thought of as a kind of Buddhist therapy. In the *Stanzas* Nagarjuna developed emptiness as a tool that monks might use pragmatically to pry themselves loose from their attachment to false views. Within a monastic environment, monks engaged in various practices, including meditation, chanting, devotional rites, and study. The principle of emptiness was one more tool to be used skillfully by the monks in their quest for freedom from attachment. If it is not a Buddhist assertion about Ultimate Reality or a manifestation of the Absolute, emptiness certainly is not a form of witness to a God that enters into the lives of human beings to transform them. Moreover, in keeping with his sense of emptiness as a religious therapy, Nagarjuna says nothing in the *Stanzas* to indicate that emptiness "happens" to human beings as an "event." Emptiness is not disclosed to human beings in a way that is akin to the revelation of incomprehensibility. Aquinas and Nagarjuna are quite different in this regard.

This difference separating Nagarjuna from Aquinas opens up an important issue for Buddhists and Christians in dialogue: the question of what Christians call grace. For Aquinas, God's incomprehensibility comes to human beings as a grace. This means that a realization of God's true incomprehensibility brings about a life-changing transformation in a human being. Recognizing God's incomprehensibility as a grace also means recognizing that this transformation is the work of God, not the result of human effort. Buddhists speak of awakening to emptiness. Can this awakening be understood as a transforming grace? Does awakening to emptiness "happen" to Buddhists in a way similar to the way incomprehensibility "happens" to Christian believers? Within Christianity, God's incomprehensibility is an event in the spiritual quest of a Christian believer. Is awakening to emptiness an event as well? And if so, what might this mean?

In the *Stanzas* Nagarjuna develops his notion of emptiness as a therapy to be employed by monks, not as an event that happens to monks. The notion of a transforming grace, so prominent in Christianity, would seem to be very foreign to Nagarjuna. Given Nagarjuna's immense influence, taking the view that Buddhism has no understanding of grace seems tempting. Buddhism is a non-theistic religion. The silence of the Buddha and the principle of emptiness can be taken as a critique of Christian belief in a creator God. The notion of grace would seem to fall within this critique as well. Taking this view of Buddhism, however, would be ill advised. The *Stanzas* do not exhaust the complexity of Nagarjuna as a Buddhist practitioner, let alone the many currents that make up the great river of religious teaching that is Buddhism. Moreover, Buddhist emptiness has a long history during which this principle underwent much development, not only in India but also in China, Tibet, and Japan.

Take, for example, the debate about awakening to emptiness that arose among Chinese Buddhists in the centuries after Nagarjuna's *Stanzas* were translated into Chinese. Ch'an Buddhists of the Southern school insisted that awakening happened suddenly, not gradually as the result of much effort. Much was at stake in this controversy. If awakening comes gradually, as the Northern school seems to have taught, then the more one meditates, the closer one comes to enlightenment. This would mean that meditation is a means to an end. The Southern school rejected this view as a subtle form of attachment to nirvana. Nagarjuna, remember, showed that even nirvana itself is empty and that the idea of nirvana as an escape from *samsara* is a false view. Meditation, therefore, cannot be a means to an end. Awakening to emptiness must come suddenly, not gradually as the result of much effort on the meditation pillow. The doctrine of sudden enlightenment provides the background to Chinese Buddhist stories about dramatic awakening experiences. The story of Hui-neng (638–713) is one of the most famous. As a young boy, Hui-neng hears the Diamond Sutra being chanted by a monk and is suddenly awakened to emptiness. His awakening is subsequently authenticated by a Ch'an master.[26] The Southern school's insistence on sudden enlightenment is a Chinese Buddhist way to recognize that awakening to emptiness is something that happens to us, suddenly, apart from our own efforts at meditation and academic study of the Sutras. The truth of emptiness came to Hui-neng in the form of a transforming event.

Similarly, the great Japanese Zen master Dogen (1200–1253) was suddenly enlightened while listening to a talk given by the abbot of his monastery. While listening to the abbot, a monk falls asleep. The abbot says to the sleeping monk, "In Zen, body and mind are molting away." Dogen, witnessing this, suddenly is enlightened.[27] My friend Shumyo Kojima, a Zen monk living in Los Angeles, normally does not use the word *megumi*, the term Japanese Christians use for grace, in our discussions. He is quite confident, however, that the truth of emptiness is not merely a logical principle or philosophical concept. Certainly, Zen does not teach that awakening to emptiness is the achievement of a self trying to become enlightened. The truth of emptiness comes to us in an event, suddenly—like "snow falling off a pine-bough," as he likes to say.

If Zen cannot be thought of as a religion of self-empowerment as opposed to a religion of grace, this is all the more the case with Pure Land Buddhism. The great Japanese teacher Shinran (1173–1262) taught that the true "working" *(hataraki)* of emptiness is "Other-power" *(tariki)*.[28] The term *Other-power* is often translated into English as "grace." There is good reason for this. Shinran likes this term because it emphasizes the transformation of life by a power that cannot be identified with our own efforts. Moreover, in a way that contrasts with Nagarjuna's view of emptiness as a therapy in the hands of a monk, Shinran thinks of emptiness as something that "works" to bring about our "salvation" *(sukui)*. If Other-power is recognized as a Buddhist form of grace, however, Christians will have to come to grips with a non-theistic doctrine of grace. This may prove to be enriching for Christian faith. Christianity's dialogue with Pure Land Buddhism, however, has hardly begun.[29]

Zen's emphasis on sudden enlightenment and Pure Land Buddhism's emphasis on the working of emptiness as Other-power seem far removed from Nagarjuna's sense of emptiness as a pragmatic therapy. I therefore hasten to point out that Nagarjuna is honored as a patriarch in both the Zen and the Pure Land traditions. There is much need for more study and dialogue in depth on the issue of grace in Christianity and Buddhism. More reflection on the "event character" of both emptiness and incomprehensibility may prove helpful in guiding this discussion.

JESUS CHRIST AND THE EMPTINESS OF GOD

The incomprehensible God of Christian faith is not the same thing as Buddhist emptiness. There are real and significant differences distinguishing Christianity from Buddhism. For this reason, dialogue among Christians and Buddhists is theologically illuminating. Even though different, Nagarjuna's emptiness may still prove to be a stimulus to Christian theology. Nowhere is this more apparent than in the lively dialogue currently taking place between Christians and Buddhists in the area of Christology, the meaning of Jesus Christ as God incarnate.

For the first several centuries of its existence, the Christian community was engaged in a difficult struggle to articulate what it meant by its belief that Jesus of Nazareth was fully human and fully divine. The doctrine of the incarnation is the result of a dialogue between Christian faith and Greek thought. Like the dialogue with Buddhism today, the dialogue with Greek philosophy produced both similarities and differences. Arguably, the doctrine of the incarnation represents a high point in Christianity's openness to Greek thought and its willingness to use Greek thought critically as a resource for understanding itself in new ways. What if the doctrine of the incarnation, so indebted to Greek thought, were to be placed in dialogue with Buddhist thought?

Buddhist emptiness may be the negation of God's transcendent otherness, as Hisamatsu Shin'ichi argued. The Christian God, however, is not simply transcendent. The transcendence of God has become immanent in the person of Jesus of Nazareth in a way that does not negate either the humanity of Jesus or the holiness of God. How does Nagarjuna's emptiness illuminate, either by way of similarity or difference, the incarnation of God in Jesus? Some of the most creative work in this area of Christian theology has been done by Masao Abe, a Japanese Buddhist and one of my dialogue partners.[30]

For Masao Abe, among the most touching and impressive passages in the Christian scriptures is the following hymn found in the Letter to the Philippians:

> Have among yourselves the same attitude that is also yours in Christ Jesus,
> > Who, though he was in the form of God,
> > > did not regard equality with God something to be
> > > grasped.
> > Rather, he emptied himself,
> > > taking the form of a slave,
> > > coming in human likeness;
> > and found in human appearance,
> > he humbled himself,
> > > becoming obedient to death,
> > > even death on a cross. (Phil 2:5–8)

Since it is a hymn, the original context of the passage is presumably liturgical. But Abe's approach to the text is governed more by his understanding of Buddhist emptiness than by the historical-critical approach to scripture.[31] The hymn sings of the incarnation of Jesus Christ as a human being, the Word become flesh in order that he might dwell among us. Christ Jesus, who is God, becomes that which is not God but rather a part of creation. The humbling of Christ is accomplished by means of a *kenosis*, the Greek word for "emptying." The Philippians hymn continues in its praise of Jesus Christ by connecting Christ's humiliation with his exaltation:

> > Because of this, God greatly exalted him
> > > and bestowed on him the name
> > > that is above every name,
> > that at the name of Jesus
> > > every knee should bend,
> > > of those in heaven and on earth and under the earth,
> > > and every tongue confess that
> > > Jesus Christ is Lord,
> > > to the glory of God the Father. (Phil 2:9–11)

Because of his humiliation through self-emptying, Jesus has been exalted and given "a name which is above every name" such that in confessing Jesus Christ, God the Father is given glory. In home in Kyoto, not far from Ryoan-ji temple, Abe told me that he sees in the Philippians hymn an opportunity for Buddhists to serve Christians by helping them to understand the path of Christ in new ways.

Christians need to recognize in this overture the possibility of developing new forms of solidarity with the Buddhist community. Abe does not believe that Buddhism and Christianity are fundamentally similar. He certainly does not believe that the Buddhist path is the work of the Holy Spirit. He does believe, however, that Buddhists and Christians can learn from one another and that this will benefit the world.

Jesus Christ is the revelation of the true God according to Christian teaching. According to the hymn in Philippians, the God revealed by the Christ is a God to which the Christ does not cling. Though he was "in the form of God," Christ does not deem "equality with God a thing to be grasped." Instead, out of self-sacrificial love, he empties himself, taking the form of a servant. In addition, Abe argues that we should think of Christ's renunciation of divinity as total. By utterly letting go of the divine, Christ becomes fully human. But after abandoning his divinity and becoming human, Christ is given a cross and then exalted in the resurrection. By dying and rising Jesus is seated once again "at the right hand of the Father." Only by means of this humiliation and exaltation does Jesus Christ become the icon of the living God, who is empty and not to be made into an obsession.

In clarifying his Buddhist reading of the hymn, Abe makes use of the paradoxical logic of emptiness in the Prajna-paramita literature, the immediate predecessor of Nagarjuna's Madhyamika school. Christ reveals the paradoxical logic of God's transcendence and immanence. The Son of God is not the Son of God, Abe argues, and precisely because he is not the Son of God, he is the Son of God. Like the emptiness of emptiness, the Son of God is not the Son of God because he does not cling to being God. Precisely because the Son does not cling to transcendent divinity and has become a human being, the Son is truly God.[32] According to Nagarjuna, emptiness that is not completely empty is a false view of emptiness. In the same paradoxical way, the God that clings to an eternal transcendence, removed from creation, is not the true God.

Thus, in Abe's Christology, only by means of a radical *kenosis* can God be the living God witnessed to by Christians. A God that does not undergo such self-emptying is but a philosophical abstraction—or worse, a god that is not the God witnessed to by Christian faith. The living God of Christian faith is the God who self-empties by becoming that which is not God (a human being). Therefore, the self-negation through self-emptying is complete only in the cross, where the self-emptying God becomes fully human by dying into God. Thus, not only is Christ's *kenosis* the self-negation of God, it is also God's radical self-realization as the saving love that has triumphed over death. Therefore, the emptiness of the true God does not reveal the universe as meaningless and godless. Only in being empty is God revealed as love.

Three points bear closer examination. First, the Council of Chalcedon (AD 451) clarified Christian belief about Jesus Christ by declaring him fully divine and fully human. Those who hold that Jesus was really divine and only appeared to be human (Docetism) are not orthodox. Those who hold that Jesus was fully human but not fully divine (Arianism) are not orthodox. In Abe's Buddhist Christology, Jesus is fully human and fully divine by virtue of the paradoxical logic of emptiness. Second, Abe's Christology demands that we not understand the incarnation and resurrection, the humiliation and exaltation of Jesus Christ, as simply sequential events within history. To do so would suggest that first Christ is God, then Christ is not God but human, and finally, after the resurrection, Christ is God once again and no longer human. Abe takes the entire drama of the incarnation and resurrection of Christ as a doctrine of God's simultaneous and paradoxical transcendence and immanence through *kenosis*. Third, Abe's Buddhist Christology is especially decisive in its approach to the Christian tradition when he argues that in Christ, God is completely emptied into creation as the incarnate Word. Traditional Christologies hold that only the Son, the Second Person of the Holy Trinity, is incarnate. This approach leaves the Father, the First Person of the Holy Trinity, transcendent, while the Son becomes immanent within the world. Abe believes that Christology is in need of development and that Buddhism may be a resource for Christians in this regard. To claim that the Father does not undergo a *kenosis* leaves Christianity with "traces of dualism," according to Abe. If God is not completely empty of "inherent self-existence," the divine can still be conceived as an object of our passions and attachments. On this point, then, Abe is critical of Christian theologians such as Hans Küng and aligns himself with theologians such as Jürgen Moltmann and Karl Rahner.[33]

Abe is the first to admit that his proposal is but a sketch of a full Christology, written in the hope of eliciting thoughtful responses from Christians and Buddhists. Abe's proposal for a Buddhist Christology has its critics and its admirers.[34] One major difficulty has to do with the historical uniqueness of Jesus of Nazareth. Since he is a Buddhist, Abe's focus is on the existential meaning of Jesus Christ as a religious symbol for Christian believers and not the historical claims about Jesus of Nazareth made by Christians. If the incarnation represents the relationship between God and creation in Christianity, the non-duality of transcendence and immanence, then in what sense is Jesus Christ also the unique historical event of the world's redemption? In its failure adequately to address this problem, Abe's Christology has much good company among contemporary Christologies. Regardless of the difficulties, Abe's Buddhist attempt to understand the transcendence of God opens up new avenues for Christian theological reflection. If Buddhism calls for the negation of the transcendence of God, there are real reasons within the Christian tradition itself for what might be termed the transcendence of the transcendence of God. Without necessarily taking Abe's Buddhist approach to Christology, Christians are required to recognize that a wholly otherworldly God is not the God revealed by the incarnation of Jesus Christ.

SOME CONCLUSIONS

All these reflections amount to only a limited exercise in comparison. Two ideas have been brought into a preliminary dialogue with each other, the Buddhist principle of emptiness as developed by Nagarjuna and the Christian notion of God's incomprehensibility, as understood by Aquinas. The exercise has yielded both similarities and differences. One significant similarity has to do with emptiness and incomprehensibility as positive statements about what it means to be human. Both principles are part of Buddhist and Christian affirmations about the human person's unlimited capacity for fulfillment through religious transformation. Significant differences were also noted. Emptiness, in Nagarjuna's view, provides a basis for imagining a religious transformation that does not presuppose a sense of transcendence as Aquinas knows it. In Japan today, Buddhists argue that Nagarjuna's emptiness should be seen as the negation of the Christian God. Certainly Buddhists are not thinking of the God of Abraham and Sarah, of Isaac and Rebecca, of Jacob and Rachel when they speak of emptiness. The Christian notion that emptiness is a mediation of the divine brought about by the Holy Spirit would be baffling to Nagarjuna and his contemporary commentators. This significant difference itself was useful in clarifying the meaning of Christian faith in a God who transcends creation. Given these similarities and differences, used carefully, the principle of emptiness can be a resource for exploring Christian faith. For example, how does the principle of emptiness allow Christians to think in new ways about the doctrine of the incarnation? The classical doctrine has been shaped profoundly by Christianity's encounter with Greek philosophy. Might Mahayana Buddhist thought serve as a resource for Christians is a similar fashion? In carrying out this exercise, Christians will be enriched and indebted to Buddhists. This will contribute in a small way to the development of new forms of social and religious solidarity among Buddhists and Christians. This is a much better way for Christians to relate to Buddhists than the fulfillment theology model.

This exercise in comparison did not take as a starting point any encompassing philosophy of religion. The discussion was not based on an a priori presumption that Buddhist emptiness and the Christian God are simply two variant ways of naming some "Ultimate Reality" that transcends all religions. The discussion did not need to base itself on a fulfillment theology either. If anything, the comparison of emptiness with the Christian God makes both the pluralist philosophy of religion and the fulfillment model more difficult to maintain. Instead of leading us back to the questions posed by the pluralist philosophy and the fulfillment model, this discussion of emptiness and divine incomprehensibility leads to the question of comparison. What constitutes good comparison? How can Christians become more skillful in learning from Buddhists?

5

Toward a New Solidarity

Herbert Fingarette, one of the great students of Confucius in the twentieth century, offered what I think can be taken as an autobiographical note in his book *The Self in Transformation*:

It is the special fate of modern man that he has a "choice" of spiritual visions. The paradox is that although each requires complete commitment for complete validity, we can today generate a context in which we see that no one of them is the sole vision. Thus we must learn to be naive but undogmatic. That is, we must take the vision as it comes and trust ourselves to it, naively, as reality. Yet we must retain an openness to experience such that the dark shadows deep within one vision are the mute stubborn messengers waiting to lead us to a new light and a new vision. . . . We must not ignore the fact that, in this last analysis, commitment to a specific orientation outweighs catholicity of imagery. One may be a sensitive and seasoned traveler, at ease in many places, but one must have a home. Still, we can be intimate with those we visit, and while we may be only travelers and guests in some domains, there are our hosts truly at home. Home is always home for someone; but there is no Absolute Home in general.[1]

Fingarette's encounter in depth with the truths of the Confucian tradition in China offers much for a comparative theologian to admire and emulate. Comparative theology does not envision any "Absolute Home in general" when it surveys the vast diversity of religions. Along with Fingarette, it recognizes the necessity of being rooted in one tradition. By retaining "an openness to experience," the comparative theologian recognizes in the teachings of another religious tradition a theological resource "waiting to lead us to a new light and a new vision." As such, comparative theology is a better way for Christians to respond to the diversity of religions than any of the candidates for a theology of religion, including the fulfillment model.

The first chapter of this book was given to an examination of the last fifty years of creativity in the development of a fulfillment model for relating Christianity, or at least Roman Catholicism, to the other religious traditions. The next three chapters constituted a limited exercise in comparison. I focused on a small corner of the Christian tradition—Thomas Aquinas's understanding of why God remains incomprehensible to the human mind even in the beatific vision—and explored it by placing it in conversation with an important idea in Mahayana Buddhism, the principle of emptiness, especially as this principle is developed by Nagarjuna. This conversation led to an interplay of similarity and difference. By means of this play of similarity and difference, emptiness proved to be of service to Christians as a resource for thinking about God in new ways.

The reason for allowing the inquiry into Aquinas and Nagarjuna to evolve in this admittedly meandering fashion was to provide a concrete example of comparison on which we might reflect in this final chapter. What relationship does comparative theology have with both comparative religion and the Christian theology of religions? How does interreligious dialogue contribute to the project of doing theology comparatively? In addressing questions such as these, we must reflect more on comparative theology itself.

Comparative theology is defined by the tension between a theologian's fidelity to a specific religious tradition and the allure of teachings found outside that tradition. Despite the fact that my most basic convictions about the world and myself have been shaped by Christianity, the teachings of Buddhism are for me both a *tremendum* and a *facinans*. Nagarjuna's notion of emptiness, for example, intrudes into my Christian worldview as a disturbing and destabilizing force. Herein lies the *tremendum*. At the same time, the Buddhist understanding of emptiness also presents itself as a real possibility for understanding the world and my Christian convictions about the world in new ways. Therein lies the *facinans*.

Comparative theologians need to resist the temptation to absolve themselves of this tension between openness to truth and fidelity to a specific tradition. Losing a sense of fidelity to a specific religious tradition indicates that one is no longer engaged in doing theology in the proper sense. Theology is critical reflection on praxis done in service to a specific religious community. When the critical reflection is no longer in service to a specific religious community, comparative theology becomes a form of comparative religion or comparative philosophy of religion. On the other hand, losing a sense of the allure of teachings from outside the tradition, or what Francis X. Clooney, SJ, has called "vulnerability to the truth,"[2] means that one is no longer doing theology comparatively. By experimenting with the truths of another religious tradition, the comparative theologian is transformed and enriched. This double commitment of the comparative theologian serves to locate comparative theology in relation to comparative religion, on the one hand, and the theology of religions, on the other.

COMPARATIVE THEOLOGY AND COMPARATIVE RELIGION

Comparative theology should not be confused with comparative religion. Since comparative theology does not seek to study religion in general, it refrains from making generalizations about religion or establishing meta-religious theoretical frameworks within which specific religions appear merely as examples. The purpose of the comparison of Nagarjuna and Aquinas in the preceding chapter was to do Christian theology, not to compare Christianity and Buddhism from some vantage point outside both traditions. As such, the purpose of the discussion was to think about Christianity in new ways, not to study religion in general or even to come to new insights about Buddhism.[3] Christian comparative theologians are rooted within Christian tradition and serve that tradition.

In distinguishing comparative theology from comparative religion, the relationship between comparative theology and the academic study of specific religions (area studies) becomes a useful question. In order to compare Nagarjuna and Aquinas, for example, I had to develop skills that in the past have not been common among Christian theologians. In order to think in new ways about Christianity using Buddhist teachings as a resource, Christians are required to learn a great deal about Buddhism. Thus in addition to being competently trained in the Christian tradition, comparative theologians must be willing to embark on a serious study of another religion on its own terms. The careful study of a specific religion helps to guard against the temptation to orchestrate comparisons such that encounters with those who follow other religious paths are manufactured to fit comfortably into Christian theological presuppositions. The work of specialists in specific religious traditions, rather than the work of those who seek to understand religion in general, is of value to the comparative theologian.

Moreover, area studies within comparative religion serve comparative theology in yet another way. In order to explore the multiple relationships between Nagarjuna's notion of emptiness and Aquinas's doctrine of the incomprehensibility of God, I had to distance myself from my home tradition (Christianity) and adopt the questions, the presuppositions, and the outlook of what is not my tradition (Buddhism). The academic study of Buddhism was indispensable in cultivating a critical distance from Christianity. Yet, despite the pains taken to locate Nagarjuna's *Stanzas* within the Buddhist tradition and analyze the text on its own terms, the comparison of Nagarjuna and Aquinas was not an example of Buddhist studies. Throughout the exercise, a commitment to the Christian tradition and to the continuing need to interpret the meaning of that tradition remained explicit and influential in governing the course of the discussion.

COMPARATIVE THEOLOGY AND THE THEOLOGY OF RELIGIONS

Comparative theology, I have said, is defined by a tension between fidelity to Christian tradition and openness to the teachings of other religious traditions. When comparison is no longer done in service to the Christian community, it is no longer Christian theology. Considerably less clear is how Christians can cultivate a genuine openness to other religious traditions. Christian faith, like Buddhism, is a highly rationalized system of symbols that constitutes a resourceful and encompassing interpretive framework—so encompassing and so resourceful, in fact, that Buddhism and the other religions can appear within Christianity's horizon of interpretation as objects fully intelligible on purely Christian terms.

This leads to the question of the relationship between comparative theology and the theology of religions.

Undeniably, theologies of religions are examples of Christian theology. The various fulfillment theologies sketched in the first chapter interpret other religious traditions from within the perspective of Christian tradition and in service to the Christian community. Also in the first chapter I criticized fulfillment theologies, not for their lack of fidelity to the Christian tradition, but rather because of their failure to meet the needs of the Christian community as it responds to the challenge of religious diversity today. Theologies of religions have no sense of vulnerability to truths lying outside Christian tradition. In fact, theologies of religions are inadequate to the needs of the Christian community today to the extent that they shield Christians from these destabilizing truths. As discussed in the first chapter, fulfillment theologies allow Christians to continue to talk to themselves. They domesticate differences by rendering them theologically uninteresting. They have a negative impact on the value of interreligious dialogue. Theologies of religions shield Christians from the *tremendum* posed by other religions to their faith. In the loss of the *tremendum*, however, the *facinans* is lost as well. The teachings of other religious traditions never are allowed to speak in their own right and never become theological resources for Christians.

No theology of religions is adequate in opening up Christians to the teachings of other religions. For this reason, I believe that, after fifty years of creative development, the theology of religions should be put aside, at least temporarily, in favor of doing Christian theology in dialogue with the other religious traditions. In this sense comparative theology can be seen as an alternative to a theology of religions. At this time in the history of Christianity a completely satisfactory theology of religions is no longer possible. In the past, Christians have tried to make sense out of religious diversity by wrestling with two basic Christian affirmations, the uniqueness of Christ and the universality of grace. Over the last fifty years, the Roman Catholic Church has moved from *extra ecclesiam nulla salus* (outside the church no salvation) to Pope John Paul II's theology of the Holy Spirit. For all its creativity and fidelity to Christian tradition, this official fulfillment theology distorts the voices of those who follow other religious paths and makes it difficult for Christians to hear what the others are saying. Today, an approach such as this is no longer adequate to the needs of the Christian community. The diversity of religions is no longer an abstract problem, if indeed it ever was. Christians know too much about Buddhists and Hindus, Muslims and Jews, Taoists, Confucians, and others. Abandoning for the present our efforts to construct a complete theology of religions will no doubt seem troubling to many. But honesty to our current situation demands it. The point of this claim is not to promote an irresponsible agnosticism about religious diversity. The point of claiming that a complete theology of religions is not currently possible is to urge Christians to redirect their energies from the construction of a grand narrative about the religions of the world to the pursuit of limited experiments in comparison. Comparative theology offers a better way for Christians to respond to the fact of religious diversity today than any of the theologies of religions.

SIGNS OF THE TIMES

Roman Catholics can now place the last fifty years of development of the theology of religions within a more historical perspective. The development of a fulfillment theology has been a part of the Roman Catholic Church's uneasy and still tentative engagement of the world after several centuries of isolation from it.[4] Enlightenment criticisms of traditional Christian belief and the anticlerical aspects of the French Revolution led to a siege mentality in official Roman Catholicism. The principle of *extra ecclesiam nulla salus* was one of the bastions protecting Catholics from the world of religious diversity. The Second Vatican Council, however, marked what Hans Urs von Balthasar called a "razing of the bastions." The council's turn toward a theology of fulfillment was one of many ways in which the bastions came down. By means of its fulfillment theology, the Catholic Church began to take the fact of religious diversity more seriously and to recognize the need to engage other religious traditions by means of dialogue.

The development of a fulfillment theology, however, must be seen as only an initial response on the part of the Roman Catholic Church to the fact of religious diversity. Undeniably, the fulfillment model has proven useful to Roman Catholics in moving beyond the bastions of *extra ecclesiam nulla salus.* Fulfillment theologies, however, must also be judged by their fidelity to the tradition and the degree to which they are helpful to the Christian community. In this respect fulfillment theologies need to be evaluated in relationship to what Pope John XXIII referred to as the "signs of the times" when he called for a second council to be held in the Vatican. The signs of the times, of course, are manifold and resistant to easy discernment. What are some of the signs today to which Christians should be attentive?

One sign of the times has to do with the flourishing of religious traditions and a new awareness of religious diversity in many parts of the world. According to various secularization theories, religion is supposed to be fading from the scene. Increases in education and economic opportunity combined with an increased awareness of religious diversity through the media and migration were to have consigned religions to the margins of modern society. This clearly is not the case. The real issue to be explained today is not the twilight of religions or their dogged persistence in the modern world, but rather the vitality of such very different religions as Pentecostal Christianity and Islam. In Taiwan, economic prosperity and increased education have been accompanied by the flourishing of a Buddhism that is both lay oriented and respectful of its monastic roots. Whether a similar resurgence of Buddhist institutions and Confucian traditions is occurring on the Chinese mainland as Maoist ideals fade is still a debated point. Diana Eck has recently argued that the United States is now the most religiously diverse society in the world.[5] Some sociologists of religion also argue that it is also the most religiously active society on earth for the same reason—its religious diversity. All these observations point in the direction of a world that is increasingly complex and increasingly diverse, religiously speaking. Roman Catholics need to read the signs of the times and prepare themselves to engage this complexity and diversity in ways that are theologically responsible and creative.

Another sign of the times has to do with the impact that global communication technologies are having on religions. Benjamin Barber is right to argue that globalization is far more than simply a matter having to do with the economic integration of markets around the world. Jose Casanova is right to note that the impact globalization is having on religions is multifaceted and ambiguous.[6] One facet of this impact has to do with the "commodification" of religion as a consumer choice. Religions are by no means immune to the power of global capitalism to appropriate, repackage, and market "tradition" as a consumer product. Globalization, by means of migration and communication technologies, erodes the traditional association of religion with territory. Islam is a major European religion now. Buddhism is an American religion now. Christianity is a Korean religion now. The secularist and consumerist ethos of global capitalism asserts itself almost everywhere.

The increased awareness of religious diversity promotes the notion of religious identity as a consumer choice. This phenomenon has a history. An initial European reaction to religious diversity was the notion that all religions are responses to a common transcendent "Reality." This can be traced, at least in part, to the European Enlightenment's need for a grand narrative to account for the "other"—including Christianity itself as the Enlightenment's "other." The ideology of religious pluralism cannot be easily separated from the colonialist mindset.[7] Now, this early modern approach to religious diversity has been given a new lease on life in late modernity by global capitalism. Like absolutely everything else, religions are things that consumers choose. The old orientalism of the European Enlightenment, with its colonialist agenda, is being replaced by a new orientalism, with a neocolonialist agenda in which the "other" appears not as a blank slate on which the West projects its fantasies, but as a consumer choice to be marketed to a public that no longer identifies with any specific religious tradition.

Religious diversity is a challenge Roman Catholics, and in fact all Christians, should welcome. The "commodification" of religions, however, is a tendency that Christians should resist. Religion as a bourgeois accessory erodes community and effaces tradition. Moreover, religious pluralism as a consumerist ideology undermines the ability of religions to call into question the legitimacy of social institutions and economic structures. Some American Buddhists, for example, are alarmed by the way in which their tradition is being made into a "brand" marketed to appeal to the "expressive individualism" of a consuming public.[8] Christian believers should take this as a sign of the times and commit themselves to finding ways to resist the "commodification" of religion as an unacceptable form of religious diversity. Doing theology comparatively, with careful attention to the theological significance of difference, may prove to be helpful to Christians and other religious believers in this respect.

In resisting the domestication of difference, comparative theologians do not stand alone. Candidates for what might be called a hermeneutics of resistance can be found among those who are calling into question the adequacy of the grand narratives of modernity. Starting with Nietzsche, Marx, and Freud, the optimism of modernity and its myth of objectivity and progress have been severely shaken. For Jorge Luis Borges, the encyclopedias of the Enlightenment have become "labyrinths of solitude." Feminists like Julia Kristeva call into question the coherence of the Cartesian subject and its quest for dominance through objectivity. Emmanuel Levinas, one of the great Jewish thinkers of the last century, speaks of the "infinity" of the "other" and its refusal to be incorporated into the "totality of the Same." In this crisis of the grand narratives of modernity, there is a renewed appreciation of difference and the contextual character of every act of interpretation. Comparative theologians should look on these postmodern currents not as a passing trend among intellectual elites, but as signs of the times with much import for Christians as they attempt to reconfigure their relationship with Western modernity as well as the other religious traditions.

The domestication of difference and the various candidates for a hermeneutics of resistance is one sign of the times to which Christians should attend. The abuse of religious difference is another. Religious revivalism can be accounted for, in part, as a response to the intrusive power of global media and the relativizing effect of religious diversity on societies that look back with nostalgia to a time when a specific religious tradition legitimized social order. In reaction to the delinking of religion and territory, variant forms of religious nationalism are gaining popularity in Russia, India, Sri Lanka, the United States, and various Muslim countries.[9] Religious revival as a defense against the eroding power of religious and ideological diversity can be seen in the Slavic mysticism of Aleksandr Solzhenitsyn and the Catholic restorationism of Marcel Lefevre, Atal Behari Vajpayee's nostalgia for a lost *Hindutva* ("Hindu-ness"), and the Wahabi puritanism of the Saud dynasty. The Christian community needs to find ways of resisting the homogenizing power of global consumerism and its domestication of difference, but at the same time, Christians need to resist religious revivalism and its fanatical assertion of sheer difference.

Doing Christian theology comparatively is a way of resisting both the "commodification" of religions and their fanatic revival. Religions are not variant forms of the same transcendent truth, contrary to most pluralists. Neither are religions so utterly different that communication and cooperation among believers are impossible. The globalization of religious traditions makes such extreme positions increasingly plausible. Doing theology comparatively can be seen as a way of resisting both of these extremes. The comparison of Aquinas with Nagarjuna in the previous chapter did not presume that Buddhism and Christianity are either ultimately similar or wholly different. In fact, similarities and differences were uncovered in a way that proved to be theologically beneficial for Christian believers. In addition, doing theology comparatively requires that Christians develop new forms of solidarity with other religious believers. This new solidarity should be seen as a way to resist both the "commodification" of religion and the intolerance of religious revivalism.

DIALOGUE AS CHRISTIAN "PRACTICE"

In the first chapter I wrote of comparative theology in terms of a shift from theory to praxis. The fulfillment model is certainly the most theologically sophisticated theory Christians have to account for religious diversity. I also wrote about the fulfillment model as a grand narrative. Constructed entirely out of the raw materials supplied by Christian doctrine, fulfillment theologies account for the religious lives of other religious believers without ever leaving the familiar confines of Christian belief. A fifty-year period of rapid development of the fulfillment model has come to an end. Now, in order to become more creatively engaged with the other religions, Christians need to shift their energies from the theory of a grand theological narrative about other religious believers to the praxis of interreligious dialogue. Comparative theology is critical reflection on the praxis of that dialogue.

Praxis is not a word often found in the mouths of Buddhists. The term *practice,* however, has a long history in Buddhism. For Buddhists, practice *(sadhana)* has to do with the need to find skillful ways *(upaya)* of making our selflessness *(anatman)* concrete. Practice is the way in which selflessness "works" for the benefit of all sentient beings. Through skillful practice, selflessness becomes a path *(marga)* for Buddhists. The idea that Buddhism is not a doctrine to be believed so much as a truth to be practiced can be helpful to Christians. Christian believers have a continuing need to fashion a life of discipleship out of their relationships with others. In a world that is "no lasting city" and "no abiding stay," Christian practice is rooted in an eschatological hope in the coming of the kingdom of God. Christians must learn how to find their own "skillful ways" to "wait in joyful hope." In this respect interreligious dialogue is not only praxis, in the sense of being an alternative to the theoretical approach to religious diversity, but also practice, in the sense of being a way to make Christianity's eschatological hope active and concrete and of benefit to the world.

Interreligious dialogue can be thought of as Christian practice in at least three ways. First, dialogue with other religious believers can become a concrete form of the church's pilgrimage toward the kingdom of God. As a guard against all forms of triumphalism, Christians need to find ways to resist the temptation to equate the church with the kingdom of God. Dialogue with other religious believers is helpful in this regard. Entering into dialogue with a Buddhist should leave a Christian with a deeper sense of Christianity's eschatological incompleteness. In his encyclical *Redemptor hominis*, John Paul II notes that the church's "self-awareness" is formed by means of interreligious dialogue (no. 11). Certainly a sense of eschatological incompleteness is an essential aspect of this self-awareness.

Moreover, interreligious dialogue is helpful to Christians in reminding them of what sometimes they forget under the influence of fulfillment theologies— that Christian eschatology is not to be confused with modern theories of progress. Christians certainly must "wait in joyful hope for the coming of the Lord," but this eschatological hope cannot be situated into any developmental or progressive understanding of history that places other religious believers on a stage as supporting actors in a play where Christianity is triumphant in the last act. In the kingdom of God, Christians will see a new heaven and a new earth. Dialogue with other religious believers purifies Christian hope of its triumphalism by impressing on the Christian believer a renewed sense of eschatological incompleteness. Buddhist friends of mine have called this aspect of Christian discipleship "hard practice." I think they are correct. Discipleship is the "hard practice" of a life completely oriented to a radically eschatological hope. Dialogue with other religious believers is a helpful way to realize this radical hope and carry out this "hard practice."[10]

There is a third way in which dialogue with other religious believers may be thought of as Christian practice. For Christians, interreligious dialogue is a form of service to the world. This insight is illustrated in a story that is both touching and revealing. Pope Paul VI, in greeting a group of Japanese religious leaders in the Vatican, read the text that had been prepared for him. Then, moved by the presence of these religious believers before him, he added a spontaneous comment: "We thank you again for your visit and pray to the Lord that we may always be worthy to love you and to serve you."[11] Dialogue with other religious believers should be motivated by a great desire for service to the dialogue partner, in keeping with the evangelical commandment to love. Thus, the practice of the church includes not only the preaching the good news and ministry to word and sacrament. Christian practice also includes a continuing search for truth and service to the world. Interreligious dialogue should be embraced as an important opportunity for the Christian community to carry out its mission of service in the world.

The official teachings of the Roman Catholic Church, however, are far from unambiguous about the nature and purpose of interreligious dialogue. Problems in the Catholic Church's understanding of dialogue can be seen in the controversy that ensued after the promulgation of the declaration *Dominus Iesus* by the Congregation for the Doctrine of the Faith. In two separate sections, the declaration teaches that interreligious dialogue is part of the church's evangelizing mission (nos. 2 and 22). Many of the Catholic Church's dialogue partners, as well as Catholics themselves, were alarmed by the suggestion that interreligious dialogue would be used as a tool to convert others to Christianity. Unfortunately, *Dominus Iesus* was not breaking new ground in locating interreligious dialogue within the church's evangelizing mission. A clear basis for the claim can be found in other official documents. The encyclical *Redemptoris missio*, to give but one example, states very clearly that "interreligious dialogue is part of the Church's evangelizing mission" (no. 55).[12] Statements such as these are hardly comforting or encouraging to the Catholic Church's dialogue partners. In spite of official statements renouncing dialogue as a covert technique of conversion,[13] confusion and reticence on the part of other religious believers should come as no surprise.

How is this linking of interreligious dialogue and evangelization to be explained? Reasons are multiple. First, some in the Roman Catholic Church still look on interreligious dialogue as a subversion of Christianity's mission to convert all peoples to the way of Christ. This helps to explain the fact that official statements by the Catholic Church in regard to the importance of dialogue are often accompanied by assurances that interreligious dialogue does not replace efforts to convert and is entirely in keeping with these efforts. Another reason has to do with the fact that, since the Second Vatican Council, the term evangelization has expanded considerably in meaning, at least among Roman Catholics. Evangelization refers not only to efforts to convert, but also to a number of other elements, including service to the world in the area of social development and "the dialogue in which Christians meet the followers of other religious traditions in order to walk together towards truth and to work together in projects of common concern."[14] However, by far the most important reason for connecting dialogue with evangelization has been the desire on the part of some Roman Catholics to affirm that interreligious dialogue is an integral part of the church's mission. These Catholics have sought official recognition that efforts at dialogue are not merely a marginal pursuit of concern to some specialists but that interreligious dialogue goes to the heart of the church's work in the world. In this regard, they have argued that evangelization be expanded in meaning to include not only the proclamation of the gospel (in the effort to convert) but also the dialogue with other religious believers. In their view, interreligious dialogue, therefore, must be seen as part of "the church's one evangelizing mission."[15]

The linking of interreligious dialogue with evangelization calls for several comments. First, Roman Catholics should be unambiguous with their dialogue partners about their intentions. Contrary to the impression given by official statements like *Dominus Iesus*, interreligious dialogue should not in any sense be construed as an attempt to convert the dialogue partner. Covert attempts to do so are not only dishonest but also not in keeping with the need to recognize the dignity of other religious believers called for by Christian faith.[16] Second, despite many official statements to the contrary, doing theology comparatively by means of the praxis of interreligious dialogue requires us to recognize that there is and there should be a healthy tension between the church's outreach to its neighbors in dialogue and its missionary effort. This tension is healthy when it is a sign of the Christian community's complex relationship with other religious communities in a religiously diverse world. Certainly, the church must not neglect its responsibility to proclaim the good news to the world. At the same time, the church must recognize itself as a community with much to learn from those who follow other religious traditions and a responsibility to build new forms of social and religious solidarity with those communities.[17]

Finally, is this linking of interreligious dialogue with the church's evangelizing mission helpful? As mentioned above, the origins of this linkage go back to a desire to affirm interreligious dialogue as an integral part of the church's work in the world. In order to link dialogue with the work of the church, is it necessary to speak of dialogue as a form of evangelization? Linking dialogue with evangelization is easily misunderstood, not only by the church's dialogue partners, but by anyone who is not familiar with this technical development within the official teaching of the Catholic Church. Catholics should find better ways to affirm that dialogue with other religious believers is an important form of Christian praxis and central to the church's work of service to the world.

FOUNDATIONS OF DIALOGUE?

There has been much discussion in recent theology regarding the need to identify a foundation for interreligious dialogue and various proposals for what Christians must do prior to dialogue in order to encounter other religious believers
honestly or authentically. Often these proposals entail a considerable revision of
traditional Christian belief as a necessary step prior to entering into dialogue
with another religious believer. Pluralist theologians, for example, typically call
for the abandonment of Christian belief in the uniqueness and centrality of Jesus
Christ as universal savior in order to be "open" or "tolerant" and above all, "ready
for dialogue."[18] This is a mistake. Jettisoning traditional Christian doctrine prior
to meeting with other religious believers does not provide a foundation for dialogue. In fact, such an approach guts dialogue of its theological value for a comparative theologian. Some examples may be useful.

Some years ago, after hearing a Christian theologian argue that belief in Jesus
of Nazareth as one savior among others was a necessary precondition for Christians to enter into dialogue with openness, a Buddhist monk asked me if this
position was a traditional view within Christianity. When I said that it was not,
the monk asked, "Then why is this man wasting our time?" Why should a Muslim devote time to dialogue with a Christian prepared to say that Jesus of Nazareth
was not the incarnate Son of God, but really a prophet in the Islamic sense of a
human being selected to "recite" revelation? Christianity is about the incarnation
of the Word, a teaching that Islam rejects. Interreligious dialogue is not about
saying things that are designed to please the dialogue partner. Using dialogue to
promote a shallow irenicism is as bad as using it as a subterfuge for converting
the dialogue partner. In both cases the value of interreligious dialogue for anyone
who wishes to do theology comparatively is lost. Comparative theology does not
begin with a revision of our theological self-understanding in order to become
ready for dialogue. On the contrary, dialogue with other religious believers is the
praxis out of which a revision of our theological self-understanding becomes
possible. Comparative theology is critical reflection on the church's praxis of
interreligious dialogue. Praxis always precedes critical reflection as the privi-
leged place to enter the hermeneutical circle.[19]

My friendship with the late Dr. Havanpola Ratanasara, a Buddhist monk originally from Sri Lanka, offers another example. Over the many years of our friendship, Bhanti Ratanasara said my faith in God was not helpful to me in the attempt
to find freedom from suffering. This is not intolerance or lack of openness on his
part. In taking this position, Bhanti Ratanasara was being a good Buddhist. Our
conversations were not based on the presupposition that, in order to be ready for
dialogue, we must significantly revise our traditional beliefs. Bhanti Ratanasara
became my friend as a believing and practicing Buddhist. He valued our friendship in no small way because I became his friend as a believing and practicing
Christian. In the course of our conversations over the years, Bhanti continued to
follow the Buddha's counsel regarding the dangers of a "mind on fire" with attachments to views like a transcendent God and an eternal soul. However, he has

also come to appreciate that belief in God, although "very difficult practice," can also be "skillful" when lived out by some Christians. Similarly, I have been impressed by the depth of compassion practiced by a non-theist like my Buddhist friend. Bhanti had little understanding of love as "the fulfillment of the law" (Rom 13:10). Certainly the idea that love is something commanded of us by a transcendent God is utterly foreign to his understanding of how the world really is. Even so, this Buddhist monk taught his Christian friends a great deal about the command to love by his Buddhist practice of compassionate selflessness that renounces belief in God as a false view. By entering into dialogue without watering down our beliefs, both Bhanti Ratanasara and I have been enriched. Our mutual enrichment would not have come to pass if Bhanti and I had revised our beliefs prior to our dialogues in the mistaken hope of making our religious traditions more palatable to one another. Skillful dialogue demands that the dialogue partners bring the full depth and scope of their religious traditions to the dialogue table.

If skillful dialogue is not based on a prior revision of Christian beliefs, neither should it begin with the imposition of Christian presuppositions onto the dialogue partner. Here lies a major difficulty with the various candidates for a theology of religions, including the fulfillment theologies. However faithful fulfillment theologies may be to the demands of Christian tradition, they tend to undermine the value of interreligious dialogue for Christians. Christians who enter into a dialogue with Buddhists attached to the view that Buddhism is a "participated form of mediation" of the saving grace of Jesus Christ and the work of the Holy Spirit should not be surprised over how little they learn from their dialogue. Fulfillment theologies, like the other theologies of religion, lower the stakes in interreligious dialogue. A Buddhist teaching, like Nagarjuna's principle of emptiness, is of considerably less theological interest to Christians if we approach the *Stanzas* knowing beforehand that Buddhists are "really" trying to name the Christian God when they use the word *emptiness*. In order to keep dialogue theologically interesting, the differences that distinguish Buddhism from Christianity must not be domesticated. To the extent that the fulfillment approach distorts other religions for Christian purposes, fulfillment theologies are not helpful as a way to enter into interreligious dialogue.

A distinction must be made between imposing presuppositions on the dialogue partner, as is the case with a fulfillment theology, and entering into dialogue as a Christian believer. Christians do not come to Buddhists without presuppositions. In sitting down at a dialogue table, Christians need to bring with them the wealth of their religious tradition, recognizing that the tradition speaks at times with many voices. They also need to bring with them the skills necessary for hearing what Buddhists are saying. In order to do Christian theology comparatively, Christians will have to gain an appreciation of Buddhism on its own terms. This will require renouncing their attachment to inserting Buddhism into a theology of religions, either a bad one like the various pluralist models or a good one like a fulfillment theology. For example, the comparison of Nagarjuna with Aquinas did not begin with imposing the presuppositions of a fulfillment theology of religions on Nagarjuna. The comparisons drawn between Nagarjuna and Aquinas, however, did begin with Christian presuppositions. The questions asked were Christian questions. The surprises encountered were surprises for Christians. The comparison led to new understanding of Christian tradition, not Buddhism. Nagarjuna's Buddhist perspective was useful in calling into question aspects of Christian belief about God and revealing other aspects of Christian belief in a new perspective. The unbridgeable differences that separate a Buddhist, like Nagarjuna, from a Christian, like Aquinas, were also helpful for thinking about Christian faith in new ways. The purpose of this exercise in comparison was to cast Christian teachings into the play of dialogue. The conversation with Nagarjuna began with Christian teachings and ended with the enrichment of these teachings.

If we must speak of the foundations of dialogue or readiness for dialogue at all, we need not talk of making major revisions in Christian teachings prior to dialogue or about a fulfillment scenario that limits and controls dialogue at the outset. Instead, we need to reflect more about how maturity of faith leads Christians to be more curious about the teachings of their neighbors who follow other religious paths and to a willingness to have their faith enriched by doing theology comparatively. Dialogue's foundation should lie in that fact that an encounter in depth with other religious believers is a genuine form of practice for Christians today.

DIALOGUE AS CONVERSATION

David Tracy, a Christian theologian, believes that skillful dialogue can be likened to having a good conversation.[20] Reflecting on his own experiments with doing Christian theology in dialogue with Buddhists, Tracy has turned increasingly to a conversational model of dialogue. When an encounter with another becomes a good conversation, we are unexpectedly made aware of the inadequacies of our views and the need to revisit our presuppositions. A good conversation produces anxiety to the extent that the encounter with the conversation partner exposes our beliefs as yet again in need of examination and revision. Anxiety, however, can also be exhilarating. This is especially the case when the question under discussion is allowed to "have its own head." The outcome of a good conversation is never safely assured. Conversation partners are confronted with truths that are not fully under their control. Good conversations seldom end with the vanquishing of an opponent, as in a debate. Rather, in good conversations assumptions are placed at risk in a mutual search for truth.

Hans-Georg Gadamer, a philosopher, uses game theory to reflect on good conversation.[21] In playing a game, the ordinary rules of life are suspended and the rules of the game are allowed to take their place. Participants in the conversation enter into the play of ideas as they arise on their own terms, with the participants not being able to control them or predict their flow completely. In a suspension of disbelief the world of the conversation partner becomes, for a time at least, another possible world within which we can see ourselves in new ways. Therefore, in the game of good conversation we lose ourselves in the play of the question itself. In order to read Aquinas using Nagarjuna as a resource, Christians have to enter imaginatively into Nagarjuna's Buddhist worldview on its own terms, at least as a preliminary move in the game. In the fourth chapter the rules of Christianity were periodically suspended in order to play by a new set of rules, established by Buddhism. The *Stanzas* was allowed to become another possible world for Christians to inhabit.

As conversation, interreligious dialogue can take the form of confrontation and debate. The questions under discussion are, after all, very often of ultimate concern. Dialogues that exclude argument and debate in the name of a misguided irenicism often become barren and platitudinous. Properly employed, a theological apologetics does not protect established orthodoxies from the destabilizing fact of religious diversity. Apologetics helps to clarify the real and theologically significant differences that separate religions. For example, Gunapala Dharmasiri, a Buddhist from Sri Lanka, offers a carefully wrought argument showing that the Christian understanding of God is a reflection of Christianity's mistaken understanding of the self. He then goes on to offer a fine argument in support of the traditional Buddhist understanding of the self, or more properly, the non-self *(anatman)*. By abandoning their understanding of God, Christians will be able to overcome their "false views."[22] Dharmasiri is looking for a response, and Christians should look on his criticism of Christian theism as an invitation to further dialogue. For the comparative theologian, however, apologetic arguments will only be occasional and preliminary.[23]

In my own experience of dialogue with Buddhists, dialogue at its best takes the form of a common search for a truth genuinely significant to both Buddhists and Christians. For example, I remember very vividly a conversation with the Venerable Karuna Dharma, a nun in a Vietnamese Buddhist lineage, who began to weep as she told us of her devotion to her deceased Dharma Master, the Venerable Dr. Thich Thien-an. The Christians present at this dialogue meeting were altogether taken up with a sense of reverence for this woman and the great truth embodied by her. Both Buddhists and Christians left the meeting with a sense of gratitude over having witnessed something of significance to both religious paths. On another occasion a Buddhist friend and I had a long conversation about scandal in our respective religious communities. How do we understand the failure of leaders and the betrayal of religious ideals? How do we respond to these failures and betrayals? To be confused, and even speechless, before a friend who follows another religious path is not a shameful thing for a Christian believer. In dialogues such as these there are no right answers and no need for apologetics. There is only humility, reverence for the dialogue partner, and a sense of gratitude for the unexpected manifestation of a transforming truth.

THE COMPARATIVE THEOLOGIAN

Since comparative theology is critical reflection on the praxis of interreligious dialogue, this theology, of necessity, must be highly contextual.[24] Doing theology in conversation with the other traditions will be contextual in two senses.

First, it will be contextual in the geographical sense of being a "local" theology.[25] A Christian theology rooted in the praxis of interreligious dialogue done in India, for example, will necessarily be different than such a theology done in Japan, or Taiwan, or Los Angeles. The relationship of the Christian community, and a fortiori the relationship of the Christian theologian, to other religious communities varies according to local contexts. In India, Christian theologians will respond not only to the current Hindu nationalism but also to India's long tradition of securing religious tolerance by asserting the transcendent unity of the various religious paths. In Taiwan, Christian theologians will encounter a monastic Buddhism very much committed to making the *dharma* relevant to the needs of a prosperous and well-educated laity. In Nigeria and Sudan the possibilities of Christian dialogue with Islam may be limited for some time to come. Dialogue with indigenous traditions may be more feasible.[26] The best place for Christians to dialogue with Islam may prove to be North America or Europe.

The local character of comparative theology means that religious traditions cannot be dealt with as abstract systems of religious doctrine divorced from actual cultural contexts and historical events. For example, Christian dialogue with Buddhism in Japan provides a different context for doing theology comparatively than dialogue with Buddhism in Taiwan and Thailand and Sri Lanka.[27] There is no such thing as Buddhism apart from the many particular Buddhist communities in different parts of the world. Likewise, dialogue with Hinduism in India is carried out in a different context than dialogue with Hindu believers in the United States. A similar statement could be made in regard to dialogue with Islam in Turkey, Indonesia, Nigeria, or Pakistan. The history of both Islam and Christianity and the relationship of these two religions to the local contexts differ in each case. The consequences are both theological and pastoral.

Comparative theology is contextual in a second sense as well. In Los Angeles, Christians are doing theology in dialogue with Buddhists, Hindus, Jews, and Muslims. These theologians are all working in the same context, in the geographical sense of the word. Urban, multiethnic, and multireligious Los Angeles is a rewarding place to do Christian theology in dialogue with other religious believers. In another sense, however, these Christians are working in different contexts. Doing theology in dialogue with a Hindu will lead a Christian believer in directions that would not be the case if the dialogue partner were a Buddhist, a Confucian, or a Jew. For example, dialogue with Confucianism leads Christians naturally to reflection on the virtues in the moral life.[28] Dialogue with Hinduism may lead in the same direction. However, Hinduism, unlike Confucianism, has a rich tradition of devotion to female deities like Kali and Pavarti. Therefore, unlike a dialogue with Confucianism, dialogue with Hinduism may very well lead to rich reflections for a Christian feminist theology of God. Not only does the specific locale of interreligious dialogue make comparative theology contextual, but the religious tradition of the dialogue partner provides a context as well.

This second sense in which comparative theology is contextual means that Christians interested in dialogue need to specialize in a specific religious tradition. Theologies of religions tend to give the impression that outside the boundaries of

Christian tradition one simply finds all the "non-Christians," as if Muslims, Hindus, Jews, Buddhists, Confucians, Daoists, Sikhs, Jains, Animists, and others can all be lumped together.[29] In contrast to a theology of religions approach, doing theology in dialogue with another specific religious tradition should impress on Christians that each religion has different truths to teach us. Dialogue with Muslims requires Christians to reflect on issues rather different than the issues Buddhists or Confucians raise. As there is no such thing as religion in general, so also there is no such thing as dialogue with non-Christian religions in general. In order to do theology comparatively, Christians will have to develop specializations in specific religious traditions. Christians need to learn the languages of these traditions and befriend those who actually follow these paths in order to learn from them.

Francis X. Clooney, for example, specializes in Hindu thought. Instead of a pluralist philosophy of religion, which constructs grand narratives about religion in general, or a theology of religions, which makes sweeping statements about the status of non-Christians as a group, Clooney has gone to India to study the Sanskrit and Tamil texts of Hinduism with Hindu teachers as a prelude to thinking comparatively about Christian teachings.[30] John Kennan, to take another example, specializes in Buddhism, and more accurately, the Sanskrit and Japanese texts of Mahayana Buddhism. A careful reading of Buddhist texts provides him with the resources for thinking about the Gospel of Mark or the doctrine of the incarnation in new ways.[31] John Renard gathers with Muslim friends regularly to study the Qur'an.[32] Each of these comparative theologians has a commitment in depth to a specific religious tradition and does not try to think about religions in general. In this respect, although they are all based in North America, they are doing Christian theology in different contexts.

By placing in abeyance the preoccupations of a theology of religions, the comparative theologian turns from religion in general and from a concern for the status and meaning of the non-Christian religions, to limited acts of comparison. Doing theology in dialogue with another specific religious tradition needs to proceed slowly by means of modest experiments in comparison. For example, the discussion of Aquinas and Nagarjuna in the previous chapter did not appeal to one of the candidates for understanding religion in general. Neither did the exploration of divine incomprehensibility begin by asserting that Buddhism is in fact the work of the Holy Spirit. We looked at a classic Buddhist teaching, the principle of emptiness, in a classic formulation of that teaching, the *Stanzas* by Nagarjuna (Chapter 3). In order to appreciate this difficult and strange teaching, we provided a background to Nagarjuna by presenting the Buddhist tradition of the silence of the Buddha (Chapter 2). Only then was this particular Buddhist teaching brought to bear on a very specific aspect of Christian tradition in relation to the doctrine of God (Chapter 4). The principle of emptiness by no means exhausts the teachings of Mahayana Buddhism. The Mahayana doctrines of "the Three Bodies of the Buddha" *(Trikaya)* or the Bodhisattva ideal offer other opportunities for thinking about the Christian God in dialogue with Buddhism. These experiments in comparison might yield rather different results than the experiment using the principle of emptiness. I hasten to add that this experiment in comparison has hardly been conclusive. Other Christian theologians need to enter into this particular conversation with Buddhists and come to their own conclusions. As more voices join the conversation, consensus will gradually develop.

NEW FORMS OF SOLIDARITY

Doing Christian theology by means of interreligious dialogue offers Christians an opportunity to build new forms of solidarity with other religious communities. Christian theology arises out of the praxis of the community and is complete only when it has contributed to the flourishing of community. In the case of comparative theology the community that is being raised up is not the Christian community alone. Increasingly, as working dialogues bring Christians together with their neighbors who follow other religious paths, we are witness to the rise of new forms of community. For example, in Los Angeles a small group of Christians and Buddhists gather on a regular basis for lunch and conversation. We are old friends, and all of us, Buddhists as well as Christians, are dedicated to benefiting one another. We are not starting a new religion. Neither do we presume that Buddhism and Christianity are differing versions of the same ineffable truth. We are, however, a community, and the dedication we show to one another expresses a new form of solidarity that is significant to both Buddhists and Christians.

What are the virtues that allow such solidarity among believers to flourish? Of the many virtues helpful to Christians in this regard, certainly the virtue of hospitality must be high on the list. On the evening before his death in 1964, Gustave Weigel, SJ, visited the home of his friend Rabbi Abraham Heschel in New York City. These two old friends talked and studied, ate and prayed together for several happy hours. Then Father Weigel had to return to his residence at Fordham University. He died while making his way home that evening. Reflecting on his friendship with his Roman Catholic friend, Rabbi Heschel writes eloquently of his belief that today "no religion is an island." Since no religion exists in splendid isolation from the other paths, Rabbi Heschel believes that religious believers need a new appreciation of the interdependence of religions. Tolerance of other religions, however laudable and indispensable, will not be sufficient in the future to ensure the flourishing of religious communities. Religious believers will have to move beyond tolerance to a genuine sense of reverence for the many religious paths.[33] Rabbi Heschel and Father Weigel were once strangers. They became improbable friends: a Catholic priest and a Jewish rabbi. In opening the doors of his home to the priest, Rabbi Heschel had to overcome a fear and suspicion of Christianity instilled over centuries of shameful conduct by Christians toward Jews. Father Weigel showed that he had learned much from his friend when, in opening his heart to the rabbi, he went beyond tolerance of Jews and made a place of reverence and hospitality within his Christian faith for the people of Israel.

Hospitality should be embraced as a virtue for many reasons, not the least of which is the fact that practicing this virtue is helpful in overcoming our natural tendency to fear what is strange. Showing hospitality to the stranger, therefore, brings us face to face with both a *tremendum* and a *facinans*. Creating a space to welcome the stranger is a *tremendum* in that the "other" has the power to call into question the sovereignty of our own worldview. In the encounter with the "other," we are confronted with another way of imaging the world that may not be easily assimilated into our worldview or reconciled with it. Welcoming the "other" is a *facinans* as well. The encounter with the "other" brings with it a potential for expanding the narrowness of our world and appreciating it anew by seeing it from the vantage point of another. Strangers have stories to tell that we have not heard before. These stories redirect our imagination and allow us to see our own, more familiar stories in new ways. In welcoming the three strangers at Mamre (Gn 18:1–15), Abraham received a blessing he never expected. In making a place of hospitality to welcome the "other," Christians should expect unexpected blessings as well.[34]

Dialogue with other religious believers is a good way for Christians to practice the virtue of hospitality. In this respect doing theology comparatively in dialogue with other religious believers is a helpful alternative to the theology of religions approach to the challenge of religious diversity. An encounter with another religion is always destabilizing to one degree or another. The adequacy of our own religious worldview is called into question by an alternative worldview. Encounters of this kind lead to various theological options. Exclusivist theologies, like Karl Barth's, try to reestablish the sovereignty of the Christian worldview by banishing the "other." In Barth's view Buddhism is merely the handiwork of the human imagination, a clever way human beings have devised to remain in "unbelief."[35] No religion can be equated with God's revelation, not even Christianity, taken as a human institution. Other religions have nothing to teach Christians. Another possible response to the "other" would be the attempt to restore the dominance of the Christian worldview by domesticating the "other." This is the approach taken by fulfillment theologies. Buddhism, for example, becomes a reflection of the grace witnessed to explicitly by Christians. Comparative theology takes a third approach. Christians welcome the "other" in dialogue and seek to develop new forms of social and religious solidarity with the "other." Instead of banishing or domesticating the "other," doing theology comparatively requires Christians to welcome the "other" as teacher and friend.

Seen as a way to practice hospitality, interreligious dialogue can be better appreciated as a form of the church's praxis. The gospel calls Christians to make a place for the "other," to welcome the stranger, and to recognize the stranger as the neighbor, the one to whom love is commanded by God (Lk 10:25–37). Christians are commanded by Christ to love those who follow other religious paths. Welcoming Buddhists and Muslims, Hindus and Jains, and all the others with humility and a willingness to learn from them should be taken as a sign of a Christian's obedience to this command. This is not to suggest that Christians have nothing to contribute in their dialogue with other religious believers or that a strong Christian apologetics has no place in discussions with other religious believers.[36] In making a place for a Buddhist in dialogue, however, Christians recognize an important truth today—that the integrity and the authenticity of their faith rests in part on their ability to relate that faith creatively and responsibly to the faith of the "other." In other words, as an act of Christian hospitality, interreligious dialogue is a helpful way for Christians to do what the gospel summons them to do.

Plato imagined dialogue as a mutual quest for a truth that leaves both parties in the discussion transformed, morally as well as intellectually. In a good dialogue, the truth prevails. In the twentieth century, thinkers like Martin Buber, in the Jewish tradition, and Ives Congar, among Catholics, championed another vision of the dialogue form. Without prejudice toward the quest for truth, these thinkers emphasized the importance of mutuality over polemics. Dialogues are helpful in that they build personal bonds of friendship and a deeper sense of solidarity among groups.[37] Comparative theology recognizes the value of both these approaches to dialogue. Not only is dialogue with other religious traditions helpful to Christians in revising and enriching their understanding of Christianity, but it is also helpful in their quest to build new forms of social and religious solidarity with those who follow other religious paths.

There is a great need for cooperation and collaboration among religious communities today. According to John Paul II, interreligious dialogue is essential for Christians because they "are called today more than ever to collaborate [with other religious believers] so that every person can reach his transcendent goal and realize his authentic growth and to help cultures to preserve their own religious and spiritual values in the presence of rapid social changes."[38] There are many examples of interreligious cooperation arising from the solidarity created by interreligious dialogue. In Sri Lanka, Christians work with Buddhists in the Sarvodaya movement and its efforts to assist villagers in becoming economically self-reliant and improving standards of education.[39] As mentioned in the Introduction, the people of St. Paul's Methodist Church in Fremont, California, have built their church next door to a mosque built by the Islamic Society of the East Bay. Because of zoning complications, neither community was able to build its facility without the cooperation of the other. Dialogue between these two communities is what began the process. The church and the mosque have been constructed on the same parcel of land. Parking for both facilities is shared. Muslims and Christians worship on different days of the week, so parking should not pose much of a problem. However, what is to be done if the feast that marks the end of the Ramadan fast *(Eid ul-Fitr)* should fall on Christmas day? If this cooperative relationship is to work, these Christians and Muslims will have to continue their dialogue with each other.[40]

In medieval Europe the legend of Saint Josaphat enjoyed widespread popularity among clergy and laity alike. Versions of the story of Josaphat can be found in the libraries of monasteries in England and France, but also in places like the Balkans, Russia, Georgia, and the Caucasus area. The legend of this saint tells a story of wisdom gained through renunciation and self-denial. Josaphat, a young prince with much going for him, decides to give up his wealth and position in order to find wisdom through living a life of ascetic self-denial. This story seems to have first appeared in the Christian world by means of a Greek version attributed to Saint John Damascene (c. 675–749), who is said to have traveled to "the inner land of the Ethiopians, called the land of the Indians." Although this journey does not seem very likely, the story of Saint Josaphat in all likelihood did originate in India. Versions of the story can be linked in a chain connecting the eastern Mediterranean with India by means of the Arabic-speaking areas, Iran, Afghanistan and Central Asia. Many scholars agree that the legend of Saint Josaphat is actually a version of the life of Siddhartha Gautama, the historical Buddha. Prince Siddhartha became a Christian saint with his story remarkably intact. Josaphat probably is a garbled Greek version of the Sanskrit word *Bodhisattva,* a title for the prince before his enlightenment. That the Buddha's teachings on impermanence and renunciation, however disguised after their long journey from India into Christendom, should hold Christians in their thrall for so many centuries is testimony to the power of this man's life to sustain the religious imagination.

In the story of Saint Josaphat we have an example of a Buddhist tale appropriated unconsciously by Christians and put to work as a resource for enriching their own religious lives. My Buddhist friends in many parts of the world are charmed and delighted when they hear of the journey the *dharma* has made from India to Christian lands. They are especially pleased to hear how the story of the Bodhisattva (Josaphat) has been of benefit to Christian believers. For all of Saint Josaphat's popularity in the Middle Ages, few Christians have ever known his real identity. The time now has come for Christians to do self-consciously what they were doing unawares in telling the story of Saint Josaphat. Let Christianity be enriched by the truth and goodness of Buddhists and Muslims, Confucians and Daoists, Sikhs and Jains, Jews and Hindus. These religious believers have stories to tell. Christians have much to learn. The world will benefit.

Notes

INTRODUCTION

1. S. Radhakrishnan, *Eastern Religions and Western Thought* (New York: Oxford University Press, 1959), 2.

2. Diana Eck, *A New Religious America: How a "Christian Country" Has Become the World's Most Religiously Diverse Nation* (San Francisco: HarperSanFrancisco, 2001).

3. See Philip Jenkins, *The Next Christendom: The Coming of Global Christianity* (New York: Oxford University Press, 2002); and Mark Juergensmeyer, *A New Cold War? Religious Nationalism Confronts the Secular State* (Berkeley and Los Angeles: University of California Press, 1993).

4. See James L. Fredericks, *Faith among Faiths: Christian Theology and the Non-Christian Religions* (Mahwah, NJ: Paulist Press, 1999).

1. THE CATHOLIC CHURCH AND THE OTHER RELIGIONS

1. Karl Rahner, "Christianity and the Non-Christian Religions," in *Theological Investigations,* vol. 5 (Baltimore: Helicon, 1966), 116.

2. For an appreciation of the Second Vatican Council as a meeting of the "world-church," see Karl Rahner, SJ, "Basic Theological Interpretation of the Second Vatican Council," in *Theological Investigations*, vol. 20 (New York: Crossroad, 1982), 77–89.

3. Thisis the term preferred by Paul Knitter in *Introducing Theologies of Religions* (Maryknoll, NY: 2002), 63–106.

4. See, for example, the work of Jacques Dupuis, *Christianity and the Religions: From Confrontation to Dialogue* (Maryknoll, NY: Orbis Books, 2002), 45–66.

5. The work of Henri de Lubac, SJ, and Hans Urs von Balthasar can be mentioned in conjunction with that of Daniélou. The work of Gustave Thils and H. R. Schlette can be mentioned in conjunction with Rahner. For a discussion of theological developments prior to the council, see Jacques Dupuis, *Toward a Christian Theology of Religious Pluralism* (Maryknoll, NY: Orbis Books, 1997), 130–157.

6. See, among others, *The Salvation of the Nations* (Notre Dame, IN: University of Notre Dame Press, 1962); *Mythes païens, mystère chrétien (*Paris: Fayard, 1966); "Christianity and the Non-Christian Religions," in *Word in History*, ed. P. Burke (New York: Sheed and Ward, 1966), 86–101; *The Lord of History: Reflections on the Inner Meaning of History* (London: Longmans, 1958), 107–121.

7. Daniélou, *The Salvation of the Nations,* 8.

8. Daniélou, *The Lord of History.*

9. Among Rahner's more influential essays on this topic, see "Christianity and the Non-Christian Religions," 115–134; "Observations on the Problem of the 'Anonymous

Christian,'" *Theological Investigations*, vol. 14 (London: Darton, Longman, and Todd, 1976), 280–298.

10. Rahner, "Christianity and the Non-Christian Religions," 128.

11. Francesco Gioia, ed., *Interreligious Dialogue: The Official Teaching of the Catholic Church (1963–1995)* (Boston: Pauline Books and Media, 1997), nos. 371–372.

12. For statements by the FABC, see *For all the Peoples of Asia: Federation of Asian Bishops Conferences Documents from 1970–1991*, vol. 1, ed. G. Rosales and C. G. Arévalo (Maryknoll, NY: Orbis Books, 1992); and Miguel Marcelo Quatra, *At the Side of the Multitudes: The Kingdom of God and the Mission of the Church in the FABC Documents* (Manila: Claretian Publications, 2000).

13. See Michael Amaladoss, *Life in Freedom: Liberation Theologies from Asia* (Maryknoll, NY: Orbis Books, 1997); Felix Wilfred, ed., *Leave the Temple: Indian Paths to Human Liberation* (Maryknoll, NY: Orbis Books, 1992); Aloysius Pieris, *An Asian Theology of Liberation* (Maryknoll, NY: Orbis Books, 1988); and Virginia Fabella, ed., *Asia's Struggle for Full Humanity: Towards a Relevant Theology* (Maryknoll, NY: Orbis Books, 1980).

14. For the pluralist model, see John Hick, *An Interpretation of Religion: Human Responses to the Divine* (New Haven, CT: Yale University Press, 1989).

15. Dupuis, *Christianity and the Religions*, 253.

16. Ibid., 254.

17. Ibid., 96–113.

18. Ibid., 254.

19. Ibid.

20. Ibid.

21. Ibid., 257.

22. Ibid., 202.

23. Dupuis, *Toward a Christian Theology of Religious Pluralism*, 347; see also Dupuis, *Christianity and the Religions*, 207.

24. Dupuis also finds support for this approach in *RM*, no. 10, which teaches that non-Christians can be saved "in virtue of a grace which, while having a mysterious relationship to the Church, does not make them formally a part of the Church but enlightens them in a way which is accommodated to their spiritual and material situation."

25. For the most comprehensive statement of Hick's pluralist approach, see Hick, *An Interpretation of Religion*.

26. Ibid., 376.

27. For official statements of the Congregation for the Doctrine of the Faith, see *Dominus Iesus*, no. 4. Also, see the 1996 document of the International Theological Commission, "Christianity and the World Religions," *Origins* 27, no. 10 (August 14, 1997): 149–166, especially nos. 4–22; and the talk given by Cardinal Joseph Ratzinger entitled "Relativism: The Central Problem for the Faith Today," *Origins* 26, no. 20 (October 31, 1996): 309–317.

28. For Hick's view of Jesus of Nazareth, see John Hick, "Jesus and the World Religions," in *The Myth of God Incarnate*, ed. John Hick, 167–185 (Philadelphia: Westminster Press, 1977); and idem, "The Non-Absoluteness of Christianity, in *The Myth of Christian Uniqueness: Toward a Pluralist Theology of Religions*, ed. John Hick and Paul Knitter, 16–36 (Maryknoll, NY: Orbis Books, 1987).

29. Roger Haight, SJ, *Jesus: Symbol of God* (Maryknoll, NY: Orbis Books, 1999).

30. Ibid., 298.

31. Ibid., 403.

32. Ibid., 415.

33. Ibid., 417.

34. Ibid., 421.

35. Ibid., 422.

36. Ibid., 456.

37. Ibid., 456.

38. Knitter, *Introducing Theologies of Religions,* 19–61.

39. Karl Barth, *Church Dogmatics*, vol. 1, part 2, ed. G. W. Bromiley and T. F. Torrance (Edinburgh: T. & T. Clark, 1957), 297–365, esp. 299–302.

40. Haight, *Jesus,* 422.

41. See, for example, Ratzinger, "Relativism," 310–317; and International Theological Commission, "Christianity and the World Religions," 149–166.

42. Haight, *Jesus*, 454.

43. Ibid.

44. Diana Eck, *A New Religious America: How a "Christian Country" Has Now Become the World's Most Religiously Diverse Nation* (San Francisco: HarperSanFrancisco, 2001).

45. The tensions between Roman officials and Asian bishops and theologians can be seen in statements made by Cardinal Jozef Tomko, the prefect of the Congregation for the Evangelization of Peoples. See Tomko's address to the meeting of the FABC in Sam Phran, Thailand, "Dialogue, Inculturation, and Evangelization in Asia," *Origins* 29, no. 34 (February 10, 2000).

46. Dupuis, *Christianity and the Religions*, 10.

47. Ibid., 202.

48. For a lively discussion of the appropriateness of human rights activism for Buddhists, see Damien Koewn, Charles Prebish, and Wayne Husted, eds., *Buddhism and Human Rights* (Richmond, UK: Curzon, 1998).

49. Dupuis, *Christianity and the Religions*, 189.

50. Ibid., 188, 193.

51. Haight, *Jesus*, 417–422.

52. In philosophical hermeneutics, see, for example, Paul Ricoeur, *Oneself as Another* (Chicago: University of Chicago Press, 1992); and Emmanuel Levinas, *Totality and Infinity: An Essay on Exteriority* (Pittsburgh: Duquesne University Press, 1968). In theological hermeneutics, see David Tracy, *Dialogue with the Other: The Interreligious Dialogue* (Louvain: Peeters Press, 1991).

53. See, for example, Leonard Swidler, *After the Absolute* (Minneapolis: Augsburg Press, 1990); and Paul Knitter, *One Earth, Many Religions: Multifaith Dialogue and Global Responsibility* (Maryknoll, NY: Orbis Books, 1995).

54. I hasten to point out that Jacques Dupuis is supportive of this project. According to Dupuis, the point of departure, at least for a theology of religions, is interreligious dialogue. A "dialogical interreligious theology," in his view, is "a new method for doing theology in a situation of religious pluralism" (see Dupuis, *Christianity and the Religions,* 11, 86). See also Joseph DiNoia, *The Diversity of Religions: A Christian Perspective* (Washington, DC: Catholic University of America, 1992), 127. For my earlier work on this topic, see James Fredericks, *Faith among Faiths: Christian Theology and Non-Christian Religions* (Mahwah, NJ: Paulist Press, 1999), 165–173.

55. See Yoshifumi Ueda and Dennis Hirota, *Shinran: An Introduction to His Thought* (Kyoto: Hongwanji International Center, 1989).

56. In May 2001, during a meeting of the International Catholic–Jewish Liaison Committee, Cardinal Walter Kasper made the following statement: "Therefore the church believes that Judaism, i.e., the faithful response of the Jewish people to God's irrevocable

covenant, is salvific for them, because God is faithful to his promises." Furthermore, the cardinal assured Jewish participants that "mission . . . cannot be used with regard to Jews, who believe in the true and one God." Kasper also makes a distinction between evangelization and mission, the latter meaning proclamation with the intention to convert (see "The Good Olive Tree," *America* [September 17, 2001], 14).

2. A MAN OF MOMENTOUS SILENCE

1. Shusaku Endo, *Silence*, trans. William Johnston (Tokyo: The Charles E. Tuttle Company, 1969), 104, 105.

2. Samyutta-Nikaya, part 4, 400–401. This text has been included in John S. Strong, *The Experience of Buddhism: Sources and Interpretations* (Belmont, CA: Wadsworth Publishing Company, 1994), 95–96.

3. For a careful discussion of Nietzsche's criticism of Buddhism, see Robert G. Morrison, *Nietzsche and Buddhism* (New York: Oxford University Press, 1997).

4. For a discussion of interpreters who have taken this approach, see A. B. Keith, *Buddhist Philosophy in India and Ceylon* (Oxford: Clarendon Press, 1923), 45; and Raimundo Panikkar, *The Silence of God, The Answer of the Buddha* (Maryknoll, NY: Orbis Books, 1990), 9–10.

5. Takeuchi Yoshinori, *The Heart of Buddhism* (New York: Crossroad, 1983), 6; Samyutta-Nikaya, part 5, trans. F. L. Woodward (London: Pali Text Society, 1979), 370.

6. For a discussion of mystical approaches to the Buddha's silence and the problems attending them, see Panikkar, *The Silence of God, The Answer of the Buddha,* 13–15.

7. William Johnston, *The Still Point* (San Francisco: Harper & Row, 1970).

8. Hans Waldenfels, *Absolute Nothingness: Foundations of a Buddhist-Christian Dialogue*, trans. J. W. Heisig (Mahwah, NJ: Paulist Press, 1980).

9. For an example of Suzuki's earlier use of mysticism for comparing Buddhism with Christianity, see D. T. Suzuki, *Mysticism, Christian and Buddhist* (London: George Allen and Unwin, 1957; reprint London: Unwin Paperbacks, 1979), 27.

10. This interpretation can be ascribed to Helmuth von Glasenapp, *Die fünf grossen Religionen*, vol. 1 (Düsseldorf, 1952). C. A. F. Rhys Davids looked on the teachings of the Buddha as a form of pragmatism (see her *Buddhist Psychology* [London, 1914]).

11. Majhima-Nikaya, vol. 1, trans. I. B. Horner (London: Pali Text Society, 1967), 426–427; and Takeuchi Yoshinori, *The Heart of Buddhism* (New York: Crossroad, 1983), 4–5.

12. For a discussion of the many traditions surrounding the life of Siddhartha Gautama, see Gadjin Nagao, "The Life of the Buddha: An Interpretation," in *Eastern Buddhist* 22 (NS), no. 2 (1987): 1–31; and Sir Arthur Basham, *The Glory That Was India* (New York: Taplinger, 1968).

13. Buddhists are generally agreed that Buddha lived eighty years. In Sri Lanka, Siddhartha is said to have been born in 624 BC while the year 448 BC is derived from Indian, Chinese, and Tibetan sources.

14. E. H. Johnson, *Asvaghosa's Buddhacarita, or Acts of the Buddha* (Delhi:Banarsidass, 1936, 1984), pp. 36–38.

15. Majhima-Nikaya, 1:207.

16. See the commentary on the Buddha's renunciation in John S. Strong, *The Experience of Buddhism: Sources and Interpretations* (Belmont, CA: Wadsworth Publishing Company, 1994), 9–10. For a discussion of the more general legacy of these traditions for Buddhism as a whole, see Gadjin Nagao, "The Life of the Buddha as Parable for Later Buddhist Thought," in *Eastern Buddhist* 24 (new series), no. 2 (1991): 1–32.

17. See the Majhima-Nikaya, vol. 2, trans. I. B. Horner (London: Pali Text Society, 1967), 9.

18. See Gary Thompson, *Reflections on the Life of the Buddha* (London: The Buddhist Society, 1983), 7.

19. See the Dharmacakrapravartana Sutra (Sutra on Setting in Motion the Wheel of the *Dharma*), which was eventually incorporated into many different early Buddhist texts, both Pali and Sanskrit.

20. *Mahavastu*, ed. Emile Senart (Paris: Imprimerie Nationale, 1857), 3:330–334. See also Strong, *The Experience of Buddhism,* 33–34.

21. For this tripod analogy, see Francis Cook, *Hua-yen Buddhism: The Jeweled Net of Indra* (University Park, PA: Pennsylvania State University Press, 1977), 13.

22. Senart, *Mahavastu*, 3:330–334. See also Strong, *The Experience of Buddhism*, 33–34.

23. *The Milendapanho*, ed. V. Trenckner (London: Pali Text Society, 1986), 25–28. See also Strong, *The Experience of Buddhism*, 91–94.

24. Senart, *Mahavastu*, 3:330–334. See also Strong, *The Experience of Buddhism,* 33–34.

25. Walpola Rahula, *What the Buddha Taught* (New York: Grove Press, 1959), 35–36.

26. Samyutta Nikaya, part 4, Pali Translation Society, 139.

27. Strong, *The Experience of Buddhism,* 110; see also Majhima-Nikaya, 1:487, 3:245.

28. Rahula, *What the Buddha Taught*, 41.

29. Ibid., 37.

30. For example, see David Kalupahana, *Nagarjuna: The Philosophy of the Middle Way* (Stony Brook, NY: SUNY Press, 1986); and Rahula, *What the Buddha Taught*, 38.

31. For examples, see Samyutta Nikaya, part 5, Pali Translation Society, 369.

32. Senart, *Mahavastu*, 3:330–334; see also Strong, *The Experience of Buddhism,* 33–34.

3. THE MIND ON FIRE

1. Maha-Vagga 1:21:1. See also Henry Clark Warren, *Buddhism in Translations* (Delhi: Motilal Banarsidass Publishers, 1993), 352.

2. For a complete translation of this text with critical commentary, see David Kalupahana, *Nagarjuna: The Philosophy of the Middle Way* (Albany, NY: SUNY Press, 1986), 10–11.

3. See, for instance, Takeuchi Yoshinori, *The Heart of Buddhism* (New York: Crossroad, 1983); and Tanabe Hajime, *Philosophy as Metanoetics* (Berkeley and Los Angeles: University of California Press, 1987).

4. See David Seyfort Ruegg, *The Literature of the Madhyamika School of Philosophy in India* (Wiesbaden: Otto Harrassowitz, 1981), 1.

5. See Kenneth K. Inada, *Nagarjuna: A Translation of his Mulamadhyamakakarika with an Introductory Essay* (Tokyo: Hokuseido Press, 1970), 3. In regard to this matter, David Kalupahana notes the tendency of later Tantric Buddhists to establish the authority of their own writings by ascribing them to earlier teachers such as Nagarjuna (see Kalupahana, *Nagarjuna*, 3.

6. Ruegg, *The Literature of the Madhyamika School of Philosophy in India*, 4.

7. Ibid., 58–86.

8. Kumarajiva is also one of the few sources on the life of Nagarjuna. See the *Lung-shu-p'u-sa-ch'uan* (Taisho 2.103c).

9. For a discussion of some of this legendary material, see Paul Williams, *Mahayana Buddhism: The Doctrinal Foundations* (New York: Routledge, 1989), 55–56. For a summary of the historical materials on the life of Nagarjuna and their assessment by scholars, see Frederick Streng, *Emptiness, A Study of Religious Meaning* (New York: Abingdon Press, 1967), 28–29.

10. See Ruegg, *The Literature of the Madhyamika School of Philosophy in India*, 2–3.

11. Streng, *Emptiness;* Inada, *Nagarjuna;* Williams, *Mahayana Buddhism*, 55–76; Ruegg, *The Literature of the Madhyamaka School of Philosophy in India*; Christian Lindtner, *Nagarjuniana* (Copenhagen: Akademisk Forlag, 1982); idem, *Master of Wisdom: Writings of the Buddhist Master Nagarjuna* (Berkeley, CA: Dharma Press, 1986); Gadjin Nagao, *The Foundational Standpoint of Madhyamika Philosophy*, trans. John Keenan (Albany, NY: SUNY Press, 1989); and idem, *Mâdhyamika and Yogâcara: A Study of Mahâyana Philosophies: The Collected Papers of Gadjin Nagao*, ed. and trans. L. A. Kawamura (Albany, NY: SUNY Press, 1991). The conflict of interpretation predates the modern period. Within the Madhyamika school itself, Buddhapalita and Bhavaviveka initiated two diverging paths for interpreting Nagarjuna. Candrakirti is generally held to be Nagarjuna's most influential ancient commentator. For a detailed discussion of this tradition of commentarial conflict, see Ruegg, *The Literature of the Madhyamaka School of Philosophy in India*, 47–86.

12. For a recent translation and commentary on the *Mulamadhyamakakarika* that also reflects Tibetan perspectives on Nagarjuna, see Jay L. Garfield, *The Fundamental Wisdom of the Middle Way* (New York: Oxford University Press), 1995.

13. Keiji Nishitani, "Bukkyô ni okeru 'kôjô' no tachiba" [The Buddhist notion of "progress"], in *Zettai Mu to Kami: Nishida/Tanabe Tetsugaku no Dento to Kirisutokyo* [Absolute Nothingness and God: The Nishida/Tanabe Tradition and Christianity] (Tokyo: Haruakisha, 1981), 150–194.

14. Inada, *Nagarjuna*, 6.

15. For a discussion of the Abhidharma and its connection with Buddhist asceticism, see Christopher Key Chapple, "Abhidharma as Paradigm for Practice," in *Pali Buddhism*, ed. Frank Hoffman and Deegalle Mahinda, 79–101 (London: Curzon Press, 1996).

16. Anguttara Nikaya, 2:38, cited in David Kalupahana, *Buddhist Philosophy* (Honolulu: University of Hawaii Press, 1976), 112.

17. The Heart Sutra is included in John S. Strong, *The Experience of Buddhism: Sources and Interpretations* (Belmont, CA: Wadsworth Publishing Company, 1995), 140–141.

18. Various translations of the original Sanskrit are available in English. Among others, see Kalupahana, *Nagarjuna;* Inada, *Nagarjuna;* Garfield, *The Fundamental Wisdom of the Middle Way;* and Streng, *Emptiness.*

19. On this point, I am following Kalupahana's view of the structure of the *Stanzas* (see Kalupahana, *Nagarjuna*, 26–27).

20. The *Stanzas*, 25:4, 7, 11, 15.

21. Ibid., 22:1.

22. Ibid., 25:17.

23. Ibid., 22:15.

24. Aggi-Vacchagottasutta, 484–485.

25. Ibid., 485.

26. Ibid.

27. The *Stanzas*, 13:8.

28. Ibid., 24:13.

29. Kalupahana observes that Nagarjuna always employs the demonstrative *idam* (this) in order to particularize his claims about emptiness (see Kalupahana, *Nagarjuna*, 85–86).

30. The *Stanzas*, 24:11.

31. Ibid., 22:11.

32. Ibid., 24.

33. Ibid., 24:6.

34. Ibid., 24:7–10.

35. See Kalupahana, *Nagarjuna*, 67–69; Nagao, *The Foundational Standpoint of Madhyamika Philosophy*, 89; and Streng, *Emptiness*, 82–98.

36. Streng, *Emptiness*, 91.

4. BUDDHIST EMPTINESS AND THE INCOMPREHENSIBLE GOD

1. Karl Rahner, SJ, may be credited with opening the contemporary discussion of this aspect of Thomas' work with a series of articles published roughly during the last decade of his life. See, for example, "Thomas Aquinas on the Incomprehensibility of God," *Journal of Religion* 58, Supplement (1978): sections 107–125.

2. Thomas Aquinas, *Commentary on John Part One*, trans. James A. Weisheipl, OP, and Fabian R. Larcher, OP (Albany, NY: Magi Books, 1980).

3. See Thomas Aquinas, *De Veritate*, 22, 2, ad. 1.

4. The *Stanzas*, 22:11.

5. Unless otherwise noted, quotations from the *Summa* are taken from Thomas Aquinas, *Summa Theologiae*, trans. Herbert McCabe, OP (New York: McGraw-Hill, 1964).

6. *Summa Theologiae*, 1, q. 12, a. 7, reply 2.

7. Dante, *Inferno* 4:42. See *The Inferno: Dante's Immortal Drama of a Journey Through Hell*, trans. John Ciardi (New York: New American Library, 1954).

8. Rahner reaches an interpretation of this aspect of Aquinas that has similarities and differences with the interpretation being developed here in connection with Nagarjuna. He interprets Aquinas's notion of divine incomprehensibility as an implicit theological anthropology that affirms the unlimited capacity of the human subject for self-transcendence into God as mystery (see Rahner, "Thomas Aquinas on the Incomprehensibility of God," sections 116–125). Reading Aquinas in connection with the *Stanzas* does lead to a recognition of the soteriological function of the doctrine of incomprehensibility, a point on which Rahner would readily agree. A Buddhist reading does not, however, lend itself to a heightened appreciation of mystery in Rahner's theological sense. For a discussion of Rahner and Buddhist emptiness, see Hans Waldenfels, SJ, *Absolute Nothingness: Foundations for a Buddhist-Christian Dialogue*, trans. J. W. Heisig (Mahwah, NJ: Paulist Press, 1980).

9. For an insightful discussion of the architecture of Ryoan-ji in relation to Buddhist doctrine, see Katherine Anne Harper, "Daiunzan Ryoan-ji Sekitei—The Stone Garden of the Mountain Dragon's Resting Temple: Soteriology and the Bodhimandala," *The Pacific World Journal of the Institute of Buddhist Studies* 10 (Fall 1994): 116–130.

10. For a discussion of neo-Platonism and its impact on Christian thinking, see Henry Chadwick, *Early Christian Thought and the Classical Tradition* (Oxford: Oxford University Press, 1967); and D. J. O'Meara, ed., *Neoplatonism and Christian Thought* (Albany, NY: SUNY Press, 1982).

11. *Summa Theologiae*, Ia, 84, 7. The text is cited in Frederick Copleston, *Thomas Aquinas* (New York: Barnes and Noble, 1955), 47.

12. Ibid., ad 3.

13. Ibid., 3, prologue.

14. For a discussion of the *via negativa* in the thought of Thomas Aquinas, see Copleston, *Thomas Aquinas*, 130–136. Nor is Aquinas the first to use strategic negation in this respect. The roots of Aquinas's use of the *via negativa* can be traced back to the neo-Platonic tradition in Christian theology and mysticism (see, for example, the *Cloud of Unknowing* by the Pseudo-Dionysius) and outside the tradition in the works of Plato (see, for example, the discussion of beauty in the *Symposium*).

15. This issue is considerably more complicated than can be indicated here. Qualities like goodness and wisdom are not to be negated when applied to God. Still, Aquinas does not think they apply to God directly. Terms such as these apply to God as analogies taken from our human experience. God is good and wise, but good and wise in a way that utterly surpasses our experience of goodness and wisdom. This issue deserves further development. One way of exploring the problem further would be to compare the theory of language present in Nagarjuna's *Stanzas* (the distinction between conventional truth and ultimate truth) with Aquinas's theory of analogy.

16. For Lovejoy's classic history of this notion and its influence on the development of the Western intellectual tradition, see Arthur O. Lovejoy, *The Great Chain of Being* (Cambridge: Harvard University Press, 1936, 1964). Nagarjuna's equating of emptiness with dependent arising itself is found in the *Stanzas,* 24:18.

17. For an account of this story, see D. T. Suzuki, *Essays in Zen Buddhism*, First Series (New York: Grove Press, 1949), 330–331.

18. This passage is taken from the *Rinzairoku*. For a discussion of this text, see Heinrich Dumoulin, *Zen Buddhism: A History, India and China* (New York: Macmillian, 1988), 128–201.

19. For historical and theological reflections on these developments, see John Herman Randall, *The Making of the Modern Mind* (New York: Colombia University Press, 1926, 1976); and Langdon Gilkey, *Naming the Whirlwind: The Renewal of God Language* (New York: Bobbs Merill Company, 1969), 31–71.

20. Rudolf Otto, *The Idea of the Holy* (London: Oxford University Press, 1923, 1958).

21. Karl Barth, *Church Dogmatics*, vol. 1, part 2, ed. G. W. Bromiley and T. F. Torrance (Edinburgh: T & T Clark, 1957).

22. Here I am paraphrasing the Japanese Zen teacher Hisamatsu Shin'ichi. See his "Zen as the Negation of Holiness," in *The Buddha Eye: An Anthology of the Kyoto School,* ed. Frederick Franck, 169–178 (New York: Crossroad, 1982).

23. Bernard Faure, *Rhetoric of Immediacy: A Cultural Critique of Chan/Zen* (Princeton, N.J.: Princeton University Press, 1991).

24. Also note that this transformation without transcendence precludes Nagarjuna from developing a doctrine of religious language in the same way that Aquinas does. In Nagarjuna, there is no *symbolum* because there is no *realissimum*. There can be no analogical predication because there is no prime analogue. However, my discussion of the *Stanzas* does not deal with Nagarjuna's notion of the "two truths" or with language as "skillful means" (*upaya*). To continue this experiment in comparative theology, one might read this aspect of the *Stanzas* with the thirteenth question of the *Summa*.

25. Cited in Masao Abe, *Zen and Western Thought* (Honolulu: University of Hawaii Press, 1985), 4.

26. For an account of this story, see *The Platform Sutra of the Sixth Patriarch*, trans. John McRae (Berkeley, CA: Numata Center for Buddhist Translation and Research, 2000).

27. For an account of Dogen's awakening, see Hee-jun Kim, *Dogen Kigen, Mystical Realist* (Tucson, AZ: University of Arizona Press, 1987).

28. For a much admired exposition of Shinran's notion of Other-power, see Alfred Bloom, *Shinran's Gospel of Pure Grace* (Tucson, AZ: University of Arizona Press, 1965).

29. For a reflection on Other-power from a Christian perspective, see Hee-Sung Keel, *Understanding Shinran: A Dialectical Approach* (Fremont, CA: Asian Humanities Press, 1995).

30. For Abe's most distinguished contribution to Christian theology, see Masao Abe, "Kenoic God and Dynamic Sunyata," in *The Emptying God: A Buddhist-Jewish-Christian Conversation*, ed. John B. Cobb and Christopher Ives (Maryknoll, NY: Orbis Books, 1990), 3–65.

31. For a well-respected discussion of this text, see Ralph Martin, *Carmen Christi: Philippians ii. 5–11 in Recent Interpretation and in the Setting of Early Christian Worship* (London: Cambridge University Press, 1967).

32. Abe, "Kenoic God and Dynamic Sunyata," 11–12.

33. Ibid., 14–15.

34. Among those who have responded to Abe's essay are Thomas Altizer, Eugene Borowitz, John Cobb, Catherine Keller, Jürgen Moltmann, Shubert Ogden, and David Tracy. These essays are included in Cobb and Ives, *The Emptying God.*

5. TOWARD A NEW SOLIDARITY

1. Herbert Fingarette, cited in Robert N. Bellah, "At Home and Not at Home: Religious Pluralism and Religious Truth," *Christian Century* (April 19, 1995), 426.

2. Francis X. Clooney, *Theology after Vedanta* (Albany, NY: SUNY Press, 1993), 5.

3. Buddhists, of course, may want to do their own theology comparatively. Although *theology* is not a traditional term for Buddhists, the idea of a Buddhist theology is attracting the interest of Buddhists in different parts of the world. See, for example, Roger Jackson and John Makransky, eds., *Buddhist Theology: Critical Reflections by Contemporary Buddhist Scholars* (Richmond: Curzon, 2000). In doing theology comparatively with Buddhists, however, Christians should not presume that Buddhists are motivated by by the same theological interests that motivate a Christian comparative theology. Other religious believers engage in interreligious dialogue with Christians for many reasons, none of which may be an interest in learning something of religious value from Christians.

4. For an assessment of the Catholic Church's engagement with modernity, see David Tracy, "The Uneasy Alliance Reconceived: Catholic Theological Method, Modernity and Postmodernity," *Theological Studies* 50 (1989): 548–570.

5. Diana Eck, *A New Religious America: How "Christian America" Has Now Become the Most Religiously Diverse Nation* (San Francisco: Harper, 2001).

6. See Jose Casanova, "Presidential Address: Religion, the New Millennium and Globalization," *Sociology of Religion* 62, no. 4 (Winter, 2001): 415–441. For Benjamin Barber, see *Jihad vs. McWorld: How Globalism and Tribalism Are Reshaping the World* (New York: Times Books, 1995).

7. For a criticism of pluralist theologies as forms of neocolonialist discourse, see the essays of Kenneth Surin and John Milbank in *Christian Uniqueness Reconsidered: The Myth of a Pluralistic Theology of Religions,* ed. Gavin D'Costa (Maryknoll, NY: Orbis Books, 1990).

8. For the notion of expressive individualism, see Robert Bellah et al., *Habits of the Heart: Individualism and Commitment in American Life* (Berkeley and Los Angeles: University of California Press, 1985).

9. Mark Juergensmeyer, *New Cold War? Religious Nationalism Confronts the Secular State* (Berkeley and Los Angeles: University of California Press, 1993).

10. In *Redemptor hominis* Pope John Paul II noted that the church's "self-awareness" is formed by means of interreligious dialogue (no. 11). The power of dialogue to intensify Christianity's sense of eschatological incompleteness can be appreciated as a gloss on this view of interreligious dialogue.

11. Francesco Gioia, *Interreligious Dialogue: The Official Teachings of the Catholic Church (1963–1995)* (Boston: Pauline Books and Media, 1997), no. 326.

12. In addition, *Dialogue and Proclamation*, a joint statement by the Congregation for the Evangelization of Peoples and the Pontifical Commission for Interreligious Dialogue promulgated in May 1991, states that interreligious dialogue and the proclamation of Christ are both part of the church's evangelizing mission (see nos. 2 and 77).

13. For a statement identifying dialogue with the church's mission but not with conversion efforts as such, see International Theological Commission, "Christianity and the World Religions," *Origins* 27, no. 10 (August 14, 1997): 114–117. Cardinal Kasper, as the curial official responsible for dialogue with Jews, has gone so far as to claim that the Roman Catholic Church has no mission to convert Jews (see Walter Kasper, "The Good Olive Tree," *America* 17 [September 2001], 12–14).

14. John Paul II, *Dialogue and Mission,* no. 13. See also *Dialogue and Proclamation,* in which dialogue and the proclamation of the gospel are presented as "two ways of carrying out the one mission of the Church" (no. 82).

15. This effort has been spearheaded, in no small way, by Asian theologians. See, for example, Michael Amaladoss, SJ, "Evangelization in Asia: A New Focus?" *Vidyajoti* 51 (1987): 7; and Jacques Dupuis, *Jesus Christ at the Encounter of the World Religions* (Maryknoll, NY: Orbis Books, 1991), 208.

16. The Federation of Asian Bishops' Conferences (FABC) has published its own unambiguous statement: "Sincere and authentic dialogue does not have for its objective the conversion of the other; for conversion depends solely on God's internal call and the person's free decision. . . . Dialogue aimed at 'converting' the other to one's own religious faith and tradition is dishonest and unethical; it is not the way of harmony." See *For All the Peoples of Asia: Federation of Asian Bishops' Conferences Douments from 1970 to 1991*, ed. Gaudencio B. Rosales and Catalino G. Arevalo (Maryknoll, NY: Orbis Books, 1992), 252. For another official statement identifying dialogue with the church's mission but not with conversion efforts as such, see the statement of the International Theological Commission, "Christianity and the World Religions," 114–117.

17. The tension between Roman Catholics who seek to promote the importance of interreligious dialogue as a priority and those who seek to reaffirm the centrality of evangelization as the effort to convert is visible in documents like *Ecclesia in Asia*, John Paul II's statement to the local churches of Asia after the Asian synod. The declaration of the Congretation for the Doctrine of the Faith, *Dominus Iesus*, assigns pride of place to "announcing the necessity of conversion" over interreligious dialogue (no. 22). The position taken by *Dominus Iesus* reflects that of John Paul II in *Redemptoris missio,* where the church's mission to proclaim Christ must be given a "permanent priority" (no. 44).

18. See John Hick, " Jesus and the World Religions," in *The Myth of God Incarnate*, ed. John Hick, 167–185 (Philadelphia: Westminster Press, 1977); Paul Knitter, *No Other Name? A Critical Survey of Christian Attitudes Toward the World Religions* (Maryknoll, NY: Orbis Books, 1985), 169–232. Hick and Knitter jointly edited a volume of essays on normative Christology as a problem for interreligious dialogue entitled *The Myth of Christian Uniqueness: Toward a Pluralistic Theology of Religions* (Maryknoll, NY: Orbis Books, 1987). For a response to this volume, see Gavin D'Costa, ed., *Christian Uniqueness Re-*

considered: The Myth of a Pluralistic Theology of Religions (Maryknoll, NY: Orbis Books, 1990).

19. For a reflection on praxis and its relationship to the hermeneutical circle, see Juan Luis Segungo, *The Liberation of Theology* (Maryknoll, NY: Orbis Books, 1976), 7–38.

20. For a useful reflection on conversation as a model for skillful interreligious dialogue, see David Tracy, *Plurality and Ambiguity: Hermeneutics, Religion, Hope* (New York: Harper & Row, 1987), 1–27.

21. Hans-Georg Gadamer, *Truth and Method* (New York: Continuum, 1993), 91–119. See also Ludwig Wittgenstein, *Philosophical Investigations* (London: Basel, Blackwell and Mott, 1958), 4–20. For dialogue in general, see Hans-Georg Gadamer, *Dialogue and Dialectic: Eight Hermeneutical Studies on Plato* (New Haven, CT: Yale University Press, 1980), 39–73; and Eric Voeglin, *Plato and Aristotle* (New Orleans: Louisiana University Press,1957), 3–24.

22. Gunapala Dharmasiri, *A Buddhist Critique of the Christian Concept of God: A Critique of the Concept of God in Contemporary Christian Theology and Philosophy of Religion from the Point of View of Early Buddhism* (Colombo: Lake House Investments, 1974).

23. For a discussion of apologetics in light of the formidable pressures to appear nonjudgmental in interreligious dialogue, see Paul Griffiths, *An Apology for Apologetics: A Study in the Logic of Inter-religious Dialogue* (Maryknoll, NY: Orbis Books, 1991).

24. For a discussion of the centrality of social context for doing theology, see Stephan Bevans, *Models of Contextual Theology* (Maryknoll, NY: Orbis Books, 1992).

25. Robert Schreiter, *Constructing Local Theologies* (Maryknoll, NY: Orbis Books, 1986).

26. For an example of dialogue with indigenous African religious traditions, see François Kabasélé, "Christ as Chief," in *Faces of Jesus in Africa*, ed. Robert Schreiter (Maryknoll, NY: Orbis Books, 1991).

27. Compare, for example, the work of Aloysius Pieris, SJ, in Sri Lanka and Hans Waldenfels in Japan. Both Christian theologians are in dialogue with Buddhism in very different social contexts. For Pieris, see *Love Meets Wisdom: A Christian Experience of Buddhism* (Maryknoll, NY: Orbis Books, 1988); for Waldenfels, see *Absolute Nothingness: Foundations for a Buddhist-Christian Dialogue* (Mahwah, NJ: Paulist Press, 1980).

28. For a fine example of this reflection, see Lee Yearley, *Mencius and Aquinas: Theories of Virtue and Conceptions of Courage* (Albany, NY: SUNY Press, 1990); see also John Berthrong, *All under Heaven: Transforming Paradigms in Confucian-Christian Dialogue* (Albany, NY: SUNY Press, 1994).

29. Failure to distinguish among the various religious traditions is symptomatic of the problems to be found in *Dominus Iesus*. Among the more troubling omissions of this document is its failure to recognize that the Jewish tradition has a unique relationship with Christianity, theologically speaking, in accordance with well-established official positions taken by the Catholic Church. For a discussion of *Dominus Iesus*, see James Fredericks, "The Catholic Church and the Other Religious Paths: Rejecting Nothing That Is True and Holy," *Theological Studies* 64 (June 2003): 225–254.

30. See Francis X. Clooney, *Hindu Wisdom for All God's Children* (Maryknoll, NY: Orbis Books, 1998).

31. John Kennan, *The Meaning of Christ: A Mahayana Christology* (Maryknoll, NY: Orbis Books, 1989).

32. John Renard, *In the Footsteps of Muhammad: Understanding the Islamic Experience* (New York: Paulist Press, 1992).

33. Abraham Heschel, "No Religion Is an Island," in *Christianity through Non-Christian Eyes*, ed. Paul Griffiths, 28–40 (Maryknoll, NY: Orbis Books, 1990).

34. For a stimulating discussion of the virtue of hospitality in relation to the stranger, see Thomas Ogeltree, *Hospitality to the Stranger: Dimension of Moral Understanding* (Philadelphia: Fortress Press, 1985).

35. Karl Barth, "Religion as Unbelief," in *Church Dogmatics,* vol. 1, part 2, ed. G. W. Bromley and T. F. Torrance (Edinburgh: Clark, 1956), esp. 297–325.

36. For a renewed apologetics, see Griffiths, *An Apology for Apologetics.*

37. For a discussion of Plato's use of the dialogue form, see Eric Voeglin, *Plato* (Baton Rouge, LA: Louisiana State University Press, 1966). For Buber, see his classic *I and Thou* (New York: Scribner, 1958). For Congar, see *Dialogue between Christians* (Westminster, MD: Newman, 1966), 56–57.

38. John Paul II, in Gioia, *Interreligious Dialogue*, no. 491.

39. For background on the Sarvodaya movement in Sri Lanka, see Joanna Macy, *Dharma and Development: Religion as Resource in the Sarvodaya Self-help Movement* (West Hartford, CT: Kumarian Press, 1985).

40. For an account of this project, see Eck, *A New Religious America.*

Index

Other Titles in the Faith Meets Faith Series

Transforming Christianity and the World, John B. Cobb Jr.

The Divine Deli, John H. Berthrong

Experiencing Scripture in World Religions, Harold Coward, Editor

The Meeting of Religions and the Trinity, Gavin D'Costa

Subverting Hatred: The Challenge of Nonviolence in Religious Traditions, Daniel L. Smith-Christopher, Editor

Christianity and Buddhism: A Multicultural History of Their Dialogue, Whalen Lai and Michael von Brück

Islam, Christianity, and the West: A Troubled History, Rollin Armour, Sr.

Many Mansions? Multiple Religious Belonging, Catherine Cornille, Editor

No God But God: A Path to Muslim-Christian Dialogue on the Nature of God, A. Christian van Gorder

Understanding Other Religious Worlds: A Guide for Interreligious Education, Judith Berling

Christophany: The Fullness of Man, Raimon Panikkar

Understanding Other Religious Worlds
A Guide for Interreligious Education
Judith A. Berling
ISBN 1-57075-516-7

A "must read" book for persons of both left and right theological persuasions. Judith Berling shows that the religiously "other" must be incorporated into every Christian's spiritual identity and that this entails going beyond learning facts about others to understanding them wholistically as persons. It is a wake-up call for those who think world religions can be taught as a purely objective study and to those who think their theological categories can be applied a priori. One cannot "know" the other except as a subject, Berling shows, and this entails a revolution in our approach to the study of the other religious traditions.

Christianity and Buddhism
A Multi-Cultural History of Their Dialogue
Whalen Lai and Michael von Brück
ISBN 1-57075-362-8

"This is an informative and illuminating tour of the history of Buddhist-Christian dialogue in very diverse settings. The authors present a wealth of information on this encounter, together with proposals for the future."
—*Leo D. Lefebure, Fordham University*